Trying to Conceive Through Faith

A Step-by-Step Success Story

How Standing on God's Promises
Allowed Us to Conceive

Lillian Day

www.TTCTF.com

Trying to Conceive Through Faith

ISBN-13: 978-0692933831

www.TTCTF.com

Second Edition

Book cover designed by Abhishek A. Naik (Makak Studios)

Edited by Daphne Parsekian

Biblical References

Copyright © 2018

Acknowledgments

GOD
· · · ·

As I prayed for answers, you gave them. As I hoped for miracles, you provided many. I love you, Lord, with all of my heart, and I am overwhelmed by the love you have for me.

I am so grateful that you hear my prayers and answer them according to your Word. As it says in 1 John 5:14–15, "And this is the confidence that we have toward him, that if we ask anything according to his will he hears us. And if we know that he hears us in whatever we ask, we know that we have the requests that we have asked of him."

Thank you so much for the gift of our son. This journey has blessed me abundantly. Every time I see our son, I see your love for me.

I am eternally grateful and honored that you have entrusted me with such a special gift. My heart is filled with so much love, gratitude, and joy.

There is nothing that compares to you!

THOMAS

· · · · · · ·

Thank you for supporting and helping me through this book-writing process. You are a wonderful partner and continue to be my iron in this life. I am so grateful that we get to share this blessing together!

KITTY

· · · · ·

Thank you so much for your support and friendship and for your encouragement and advice. I am so blessed to call you my friend.

Be a part of the
Through Faith community

The TTCTF Community is growing every day and we want you to be apart of it!

We go through the entire book together, digging even deeper into the promises and principals in God's Word!

Come join us at www.ttctf.com

TABLE OF CONTENTS

EXTRAS
• • • • • • •

www.TTCTF.com

INTRODUCTION

It took me seven years to get pregnant. The roller coaster of uncertainty crushed me more times than I would like to admit. As a believer, this left me confused, mad, frustrated, and heartbroken.

What you will discover from reading this book is how God showed me what I needed to do to seek him consistently while trying to and eventually getting pregnant.

In this book I share actionable steps I followed while seeking God for this miracle. These steps allowed me to draw closer to God and lean on him to stand in faith and receive the gift of our son.

While I am on the other side of this struggle now, the battle my husband and I went through to get here was long and painful. I want you to know, if you are struggling right now, that God knows. He knows the heartache you have endured, and he cares. I pray in the name of Jesus that this book helps reveal God's plan for you and your conception story.

It is an honor for me to share our conception story with you. I pray by sharing this story it helps your faith grow and turns your heartache into a testimony of conception.

I also want you to know that by sharing my story with you, I am sharing my flaws in the hopes it genuinely helps you. Some steps are rough and may seem like mountains to climb, while others may seem to have no relevance to you, but they are there for you to prayerfully consider. Each step has a clear purpose and is aligned with God's Word.

I use many scriptures to back up this journey because I believe God's Word is the lamp at our feet, guiding us in this life.

Hebrews 4:12 says, "For the Word of God is living and active, sharper than any two-edged sword, piercing to the division of soul and of spirit, of joints and of marrow, and discerning the thoughts and intentions of the heart." The phrase "living and active" in this scripture makes the Word relevant to us in our time of unfulfilled promises. It shows us that the Bible is full of promises we can hope for today, not just when it was written.

I am proof that the broken heart can be mended, love can be restored, and God answers prayers.

> "Praise be to the God and Father of our Lord Jesus Christ, **the Father of compassion and the God of all comfort, who comforts us in all our troubles**..."
>
> 2 Corinthians 1:3–4 (NIV)

It is through great joy that I get to share this testimony with you and pray it brings you comfort and hope while you are Trying to Conceive Through Faith.

GETTING STARTED

I recommend reading one chapter per week to focus and work on each topic.

Be sure to check out the TTCTF Journal which is a companion to this book. The Journal also reveals how to dig deeper into the contents of this book and God's Word.

To go through this book with me and others going through infertility, be sure to join the Through Faith community at ttctf.com.

Chapter 1

RENEWED HOPE

For as long as I can remember, I wanted to be a mother. I would dream of having a large family and never considered it would not be a possibility. So first came love, then came marriage, then… well, there was no baby in my baby carriage.

As almost seven years passed, I struggled with this reality. I prayed for God to tell me if it was his will for us to have children or not. I prayed every month that somehow "this month" would be "the month" we would get pregnant. I prayed for anything I peed on to turn positive!

My hopes were met with silence and an empty womb. This built uncertainty in me, along with frustration and resentment.

I was so desperate to have children that every month I somehow convinced myself, even with my period, I could somehow be pregnant. This hope threw out all rational thinking. I would even believe I was nine months pregnant! Even as I said it, I knew I was being crazy, but I was so hopeful we would have children that I did not care. I knew I served a big God and he was capable of anything, so why not be a little crazy?

The hope I had each month became too painful.

I stopped wanting because the disappointment was too hard, and I started focusing on life without kids.

I finally chose to completely eliminate hope and face a childless life. From this new perspective I realized there are some benefits to not having kids. I even got excited thinking about the freedom my husband and I would have. Never being tied down, not having to worry about those difficult conversations about bullies, puberty, screen time, and so many other challenges parents are faced with. I literally never thought about avoiding all of these challenges before.

For the first time in my life, I thought of the up sides to not having kids and skipping all of the challenges that come along with parenting and raising a tiny, dependent human.

And with that in mind, I was happy. The end…

Well, not really. That would not be a great story to tell.

Honestly, in my "happiness," I never said I did not want kids. I was settling and trying to make the best of it, all the while convincing myself that I was happy.

Until...

One day I realized there was a chance, the timing could line up, and I might be pregnant without even trying! I got so excited again, and all of my craziness came roaring back.

I was obsessed over any and every sign. I am talking about crazy signs, like thinking everything I smelled was my new "sixth sense" kicking in. I even hoped for hardcore morning sickness just so I could get confirmation I was pregnant before the two-week wait was over.

Those two weeks were painfully long. Each day seemed unending, and I could not fill my mind with any other thought than wanting to confirm that I was finally pregnant.

In my impatience, I even tried to figure out if I was pregnant sooner than the pregnancy test would reveal. I researched information about urine to try to calculate a scientific formula in order to not have to wait two whole weeks to get my BFP (Big Fat Positive)!

Since I am not actually a scientist, I was unable to find a solution for faster pregnancy test results.

So the two-week wait lasted, you guessed it, two weeks.

When my period was due, sure enough, a spot of blood appeared. Just a spot...and I decided it looked more brown than red. I convinced myself it was implantation bleeding. I kept checking... but nothing. Until another spot...and then another and another.

Then there was no denying. I had my full-blown period.

I thought I was done with this hopeful anticipation, so I got angry because I was "happy" to put that hope aside. This month made me fully aware that my forced happiness was hiding my broken heart.

That period confirmed I truly wanted all of the blessings and challenges of being a parent. All the justifications I made to stop TTC (Trying to Conceive) were just excuses for trying to be content in a frustrating situation.

What I discovered from this revelation was that I had lost sight of God in my frustration and hopelessness and ultimately lost faith in him to answer this prayer. Facing my pain again made me realize it was time to figure out how to restore hope and faith in God if I ever expected to get pregnant.

Thankfully, God showed me how to repair my relationship with him through revelations in the Bible. If we obey his Word, we can receive all of the blessings God promises us in the Bible.

Psalm 37:4–8 says, "Delight yourself in the LORD, and he will give you the desires of your heart. Commit your way to the LORD; trust in him, and he will act. He will bring forth your righteousness as the light, and your justice as the noonday. Be still before the LORD and wait patiently for him; fret not yourself over the one who prospers in his way, over the man who carries out evil devices! Refrain from anger, and forsake wrath! Fret not yourself; it tends only to evil."

This scripture talks about delighting, committing, trusting, waiting, not fretting, and not being angry. If we have faith in God and obey this scripture in its entirety, God will give us the desires of our hearts.

I had a lot of work to do in order to align my heart and mind with the verses in Psalm 37.

With all of this work ahead, I found Hebrews 11:6 to help me get started, which says, "And without faith it is impossible to please him, for whoever would draw near to God must believe that he exists and that he rewards those who seek him."

If we want the reward of pregnancy (Psalm 127:3), faith in God is our only option. If we have faith, we can eliminate the doubt, anger, and frustration which are separating us from God. If we choose not to have faith, the Bible says in Romans 14:23 that it is sin, "For whatever does not proceed from faith is sin."

If we expect God to bless us, we have to trust him through our frustrations. We may not have all of the answers, but he does. It is time for us to prioritize faith while we are TTC.

When our faith grows, our relationship with God becomes stronger. As we continue to seek God, he will draw near to us and we will have a clearer understanding of how to honor God as we are TTCTF (Trying to Conceive Through Faith).

REFLECTION AND PRAYER TIME
· ·

1. Renewing Hope Through Faith

If hope is your enemy and frustration is controlling your emotions, then you are right where I was. Thankfully, our God brings revelation so we can make changes that line up with his Word. By reading this book, you have committed to add faith while you are TTC, and that is the biggest, most important change you can make.

2. Seeking God For Answers

Commit to reading this book.

Highlight the scriptures then read them in context in the Bible and pray for revelation.

I know life is busy and time slips by, but if you truly want to receive the blessings God's Word has in store for you, then you need to commit to the process.

Each chapter has reflection and prayer time to encourage you to seek God for the answers while TTCTF.

PRAYER

• • • • • • •

God, you know how badly I want a baby. My soul is aching, and my body feels incomplete. My life feels incomplete. My hope is dried out, my heart is throbbing, and this emptiness is echoing into every area of my life.

I have been trying to make my body do what you designed it to do, and I have come up empty. I feel like I have failed; my body has failed.

I now see the hope I have had and the plans I have made require more of you.

I will no longer put my hope, my faith, and my trust in this body; they are now completely in you. You are the God who parted the Red Sea for safe passage. You closed the mouth of the lions for Daniel. You are the God who made Shadrach, Meshach, and Abednego untouchable in the fiery furnace. You are the God who delivered food in the desert. You, God, have made water flow from a stone. You have made blind men see. You have raised men from the grave. You continually show us life where there is death. You, oh God, are the God of miracles, and you are certainly the God who opens the womb of the barren woman.

There is nothing outside of your reach; there is nothing you cannot make whole. Every mountain I face is nothing compared to your greatness.

Please forgive me for my frustration and emptiness.

Please remove this brokenness.

Please let me be filled with your love and peace.

Please show me how to grow my faith.

I believe, God, that you hear my prayers, and I know without a doubt you are capable of answering them. Today I ask you to reveal why you have not answered this prayer.

I know your love for me is so great that no matter how many times I fail, you are there to pick me up. You are the God of love and of mercy, and I need them both.

I will no longer try to conceive without faith; my faith is in you. Today is a new start, a new beginning that you have given me. I will seek you for answers and wait for your direction.

Today my faith and hope are restored in you.

Thank you, God, for your faithfulness!

In Jesus' name,
Amen

Chapter 2

CONQUERING FEAR

Now that I realized I had been lying to myself in order to force happiness, it became clear to me that I could not do this alone. Even my renewed hope did not change the fact that I still was not pregnant.

So I was back in baby mode. This time around, I started seriously considering what was wrong. Nothing about my husband or myself was off from a biological standpoint. After years of not officially being ready, we were finally in agreement to actively start TTC, but for some reason, it was not working. Year after year, our situation grew harder because our prayers and hopes were not being answered.

In my renewed hope, I realized something had to change.

We could not keep doing the same thing if we wanted to get a different result. No wonder I felt like I was going crazy—I was following the definition of insanity. In order to change the outcome, something had to be different. Since God is the same and does not change (Malachi 3:6), this meant I was the one who needed to make changes.

As I prayed for God to show me what to do differently, he put this question on my heart: "Why am I afraid of having kids?" I prayerfully reflected on this question and realized I had a lot of different fears associated with having children.

No single fear surprised me, but the number of items collectively made me realize this was a bigger problem than I had realized. I could probably write a book just about those fears, but fear can spread, and I do not want to suggest additional fears by sharing them here.

I was overwhelmed by the quantity of my fears. I am not a fearful person—at least I did not think I was. So, for a while, I hung onto those fears; I let them echo in my mind and even validate my situation.

But one day I had a revelation that was so profound and simple yet brought so much clarity that it literally gave me freedom from all of my fears.

You are going to laugh (or roll your eyes) at how simple this is because it is something we all know as believers and something I have known since I gave my life to the Lord. Somehow I tucked this knowledge away, so when fears were in focus, this one fact was just out of reach until God revealed it to me again.

God showed me that my husband and I were not alone. God revealed that he is not only with us but guiding us, protecting us, and lighting the path at our feet (Psalm 119:105).

This was all confirmed in Joshua 1:9, which says, "Have I not commanded you? Be strong and courageous. Do not be frightened, and do not be dismayed, for the LORD your God is with you wherever you go." This revelation gave me freedom!

The shackles of fear had been released. If God is with me, then no fear is justifiable, no mountain is unconquerable, and no lie is believable.

Deep in my heart, I knew God was always there, but I became comfortable without his help. I was so comfortable that I forgot the Lord is more than just there; he is a present and active part of our lives if we let him be.

Any doubt I had about God answering this prayer washed away because my fears were gone. The fear the enemy used to steal the joy of motherhood was released. There was no longer a foothold on this part of my life. I was now filled with joy, hope, and the excitement of having children.

The truth is, without the Lord, we really are alone, fending for ourselves. If we choose, God will let us wander in the darkness until we reach out and ask for his light at our feet.

But we wont see how God is guiding us if we are living in fear. Fear takes away from our faith and puts our focus on it instead of on God. I realized that as my fears grew, my faith shrunk. I became less reliant on God and more absorbed in the broken abandonment I felt. Instead of allowing the Lord to help me, I relied on myself and got nowhere.

This revelation allowed me to stop relying on myself and to trust God completely in getting pregnant and raising children. I no longer had pressure to do everything perfectly, because the weight was no longer loaded on my shoulders.

What is amazing about having a revelation is, it happens instantly. Previously you could not see something, but now you can. It might be very plain and obvious to everyone else, but it is not less meaningful when God reveals it to you. My revelation was simple. I even laugh now because it was not new information to me, but I received it in a new way, which gave me peace.

With my fears revealed, they could no longer be used against me, because I focused on trusting God and his faithfulness instead. As soon as a fear arose, I would repeat 2 Timothy 1:7, reminding myself those fears are not from the Lord. They are a lie I would no longer be a slave to.

Second Timothy 1:7 says, "for God gave us a spirit not of fear but of power and love and self-control."

John 14:27 (NIV) shows us that we can have peace instead of fear: "Peace I leave with you; my peace I give you. I do not give to you as the world gives. Do not let your hearts be troubled and do not be afraid."

This peace made all of my fear irrelevant. My faith grew in the Lord, and my hope was renewed. The pain and scars from previous years washed away, and I finally accepted help from God instead of living in fear.

After being gifted with this revelation, I needed to make sure I would not forget again. I had to dig deeper to find out why I allowed myself to forget that God was always there to help, protect, and guide me.

As I continued to prayerfully search my heart, I realized I was conditioned to be self-reliant from childhood. This independence was certainly a part of my personality, but it grew to become a necessity that was ingrained into my thought process. My independence and self-reliance followed me into my relationship with God.

I started excluding the Lord from little things, and the exclusion grew into bigger and more important areas of my life. Eventually I had taken back the reins on my life and was blindly leading myself into the fruitless situation that left me bitter, resentful, and angry.

Leaving God out of the equation cascaded into years of a drought in my walk with the Lord. I never turned my back on God, but I know I missed out on his blessings. I spent years wandering in darkness. All I had to do was be obedient to him and open up his Word, which is the lamp at our feet (Psalm 119:105) to guide us, but I chose to ignore that direction.

My childhood perspective affected my adult relationship with the Lord. With each negative pregnancy test, I believed the lie that I was alone and had to fend for myself. Through revelation and good counsel, I was able to distinguish between the lie and the truth the Lord had promised me.

I finally found freedom from the lies I had been repeating in my head. Even before I accepted God into my life, he was always there and always will be. This initial revelation is what began my journey of renewing my faith in him, which ultimately allowed us to get pregnant.

We have a choice to either lean on ourselves or lean on God with all things, including TTC. If we choose to hold onto our fears, we are not trusting God fully. If we want to receive peace and freedom, we have to address our fears so we can trust and depend on God.

REFLECTION AND PRAYER TIME

1. Revelation of Fear

Fear needs to be addressed. Prayerfully ask yourself if you have fears that are taking away from your faith. If you seek God, he will reveal what you need to work on so your faith is not hindered.

2. Finding The Root of Your Fear

You may have one fear or multiple fears, but there is a reason behind your fears. Pray for revelation about why you have those fears. Even if they are justifiable, God is bigger than all of our worst nightmares.

Once your fears are revealed, you can fight against them better by knowing why you have them.

3. Resolving Your Fears

Fear takes away from our faith, but God makes our fears obsolete. We have to replace fear with trust in God for every circumstance!

Second Timothy 1:7 says, "for God gave us a spirit not of fear but of power and love and self-control." You can be confident fear is not what the Lord wants in your heart, in your decision making, or in your life.

Resolving fears can finally give you joy,
peace, and freedom by having faith in the
Lord's protection, guidance, and plan.

PRAYER
· · · · · · ·

God, I thank you for your love and your protection over my life.
I have been broken for too long and see that I need to give you
back control.

Please search my heart and reveal areas I need to work on.

Please give me the spirit of wisdom and discernment to better
understand the sin in my life so I can honor you.

I know fear is controlling and can distort my relationship with
you. I do not want to give the devil a foothold anymore.

Please forgive me, Lord, for dishonoring you with my fears and
my anger about not having children yet. I know you are bigger
than any obstacle, and I realize that as my faith grows, so will
my relationship with you.

I pray specifically about having children.

I know it does not matter what a doctor says or how long we
have been trying. My faith is not in my doctors or in my past; my
faith is in you alone. Since you created the heavens, the earth,
and the process of procreation, I know and believe in my heart
that through faith, you will hear and answer my prayers with a
healthy, happy baby.

Today is a new beginning, and I am grateful you have started me
on this journey of faith.

I give you all the honor and praise.

In Jesus' name,
Amen

Chapter 3

WAITING

I wasted a lot of time waiting on the Lord without acting.

When we seek God for one of his promises to be fulfilled and it does not happen, it is easy to feel hopeless and powerless as we wait for the answer.

When TTC with and without faith, there is only so much in our control. We can figure out the right date, temperature, time of day, food to eat, and more, but we cannot actually force a baby to be created. That gift has to come from the Lord. So it is easy to feel as though there is nothing more we can do but wait.

Thankfully, there is more we can do.

Waiting for an answered prayer is not the same as waiting for everyday things. We wait in line, we wait for food to be ready, and we wait because these things take time to be fulfilled. However, God answers prayers based on our walk with him, he does not need time to fulfill our prayer requests.

So instead of hopelessly waiting for God to answer our prayers, we have to be filled with hope and take action as we wait.

What God revealed to me as I pursued him for conception was that while I was waiting on him, he had been waiting on me.

Isaiah 30:18 shows us that God waits: "Therefore the LORD waits to be gracious to you, and therefore exalts himself to show mercy to you..."

If God is waiting, what is he waiting for? It is our job to find out, and we can do so by looking to the Word for answers. Psalm 119:105 says, "Your word is a lamp to my feet and a light to my path." This scripture is very important because it explains how to see the perfect plan God has for us in our lives. It is a reminder that darkness surrounds us, but God will help light our path through his Word.

For a long time I felt a distance between myself and the Lord. That separation was because I forgot this is a two-way relationship. If we want God's guidance, we have to be in his Word. The Bible is where we find instructions and the promises God has given us. James 4:8 says, "Draw near to God, and he will draw near to you."

We have to earnestly seek God if we want to be closer to him. By faith we can stand on his Word and believe Hebrews 10:23 without wavering: "Let us hold fast the confession of our hope without wavering, for he who promised is faithful."

If our faithful God is not answering our prayers, we need to evaluate our walk with him. Now is our opportunity to draw near to God and trust his faithfulness to guide us.

In order to draw near to God I decided to start reading a book about faith-based childbirth. It was packed with scripture and faith-building truths which helped me reconnect with the Lord. The scriptures built my faith and helped me focus on the area that I struggled with most: getting pregnant.

What I discovered about faith is, when it grows in one area of our lives, it overlaps into other areas too. My confidence in God's Word grew, which deepened my trust and faith in him.

I read the book alone and then asked my husband if he would read it with me. We began to read a chapter each night. It opened up communication about where we both stood in our faith and what we hoped for in regards to getting pregnant. Being unified as one strengthened our faith, together. There is a joy that comes from growing together in the Lord. It is an overwhelming blessing that we received while on our journey of TTCTF.

As we grew together Deuteronomy 7:14 was a major faith-building scripture, which says, "You shall be blessed above all peoples. There shall not be male or female barren among you or among your livestock." Based on this scripture, I knew it did not matter that I had not been able to get pregnant yet. I knew being barren was not a challenge for the Lord. I did not have to wait for God to figure out how to answer our prayers.

After this revelation, I was faced with another question: "Since I know God can answer this prayer, what is he waiting for?" I realized through prayer that he was waiting for me. I was the variable in this relationship; God was the constant.

Malachi 3:6 (NIV) tells us, "I the LORD do not change."

It was very clear now that I needed to do more. I did not want to be the reason why God was not answering our prayers. I decided, while TTCTF, to look for reasons why God was waiting on me. I needed to dig deeper and actively seek God. Since God designed us to conceive, I also prayerfully asked, "Why isn't he blessing us?"

In the remaining chapters, I share the specific revelations God gave to me regarding these two questions.

I hope and pray the direction God gave me will help you dig deeper and reveal why God may be waiting on you. Through revelation you can address these issues like I did and receive all God has planned for you.

REFLECTION AND PRAYER TIME

· ·

1. Read the Word.

Let the Lord light your path through his Word (Psalm 119:105). It took me way too long to understand the power of God's Word because I did not know what to read. I either read the same scriptures over and over or what I read did not seem relevant to me.

I have found it effective to use a Bible app with reading plans. I began to bookmark and organize the scriptures that spoke to me. In a very short time, I discovered many scriptures I could turn to for help because I was reading relevant parts of the Bible.

Another suggestion is to read the entire Bible from start to finish. As overwhelming as it sounds, it has been a huge eye opener for me to see the Word in context instead of just pieces of stories. While it is a challenge, it is well worth it. You can even listen to it in some apps.

2. Memorize the Word.

The Bible is the living Word of God. Hebrews 4:12 says, "For the word of God is living and active, sharper than any two-edged sword, piercing to the division of soul and of spirit, of joints and of marrow, and discerning the thoughts and intentions of the heart."

Psalm 119:11 says, "I have stored up your

word in my heart, that I might not sin against you."

Memorizing scripture gives us an immediate defense against fear, doubt, anger, and more. It is a way to quickly access God's instructions for our lives so when something is outside of his will, we do not linger in lies or deceit. Rather, we stand on his Word, knowing it is the truth and lamp to our feet which gives us power over the enemy and our own doubts and fears.

Start with short, meaningful scriptures. Do not feel like you have to memorize the whole Bible. Even one scripture can give you immediate peace when fears or doubts arise.

3. Pray about these questions.

Prayerfully ask God these two questions, and do not stop until you get answers.

- Is God waiting on me to answer this prayer?

- Why isn't God blessing us?

God has answers to these questions, but you have to seek him for the answers. As you pray and read the Bible, he will answer you.

PRAYER

· · · · · · ·

God, I have been deceived in the time I have spent waiting. I know my patience has been tested and run out. Now I am faced with the question "Have I done enough?" Have I taken this time to search you, to draw near to you, and to be committed to you no matter what your answer to my prayer is? I am so sad to say I have not. I have failed in my commitment to you.

I have been frozen, waiting for an answer, and I do not believe this is what you want from me. I know you want a personal relationship with me. You want me in your Word and praying to you daily. You want me to seek you in the good times and the bad times. This time has been a trial, and I need your help. I need more of you.

If this time of waiting shows me one thing, please let it be that you are the answer to everything I need. Not time or science. Just you, God.

I will no longer wait and do nothing. I will use this time to draw near to you. I believe if I am in your Word, I will understand you more. I will hear more from you, and I will know how to be in your will so you can answer this prayer of pregnancy.

No one in the world knows me like you do, God. Please help me to make my ways your ways; help me search for you more than I have for this pregnancy.

Please show me what to do as I wait for you to answer this prayer so you do not have to wait to bless me any longer.

I love you, Lord!

In Jesus' name,
Amen

Chapter 4

THROUGH FAITH
(TTCTF)

Second Timothy 2:13 says, "if we are faithless, he remains faithful—for he cannot deny himself."

When we fully recognize God's faithfulness, we are forced to face our shortcomings. Our faithlessness shows up in doubting, questioning, arguing, rebelling, ignoring, and fighting God.

Thankfully, he does not give up on us.

Recognizing my fear was only part of my problem, I struggled a lot with hope over the years too. For a long time I felt hope was my enemy because I was constantly disappointed by my hopes never being met. I later realized, the hope I had was disappointing because it was not in the Lord.

In 1 Corinthians 15:32 (NIV) we are reminded that our human hopes are not enough, "If I fought wild beasts in Ephesus with no more than human hopes, what have I gained?" Our hope has to be bigger than ourselves and our abilities; it has to be in God.

The great news is, no matter how long we have misplaced hope, it can be restored and strengthened through God. This means we can endure this journey with hope. Isaiah 40:31 (NIV) says, "but those who hope in the LORD will renew their strength. They will soar on wings like eagles; they will run and not grow weary, they will walk and not be faint." If we misplace our hope, we will not be strong enough to endure this season.

Renewed in faith, my hope was now strengthened in the Lord, and I found renewed joy in genuine hope. Not false hope or lies but rather hope in the truth and promises the Lord has given us in his Word.

Two months passed since renewing and working on increasing our faith. We continued TTCTF.

At first, we prayed generally to get pregnant. When we did not become pregnant right away, our faith grew.

The next month, we prayed more specifically to get pregnant in the same month. We realized the details matter when praying for God's blessings. Our faith grew immensely as we prayed for such a specific detail that we missed the previous month. We were no longer hoping for someday to get pregnant; we were hoping it would happen in the immediate future. My husband and I had complete faith that God would answer our prayers.

This month of TTCTF was different. There was a calmness, not a feeling of urgency to know before it was time. I stopped looking for signs and symptoms to predetermine if I was pregnant. This calmness was peace that was backed by faith. When I felt my old, frantic, uncertain emotions creep back up, I would focus on the promises he gave us in the Bible and regain the confidence that he would bless us.

As the days grew closer, I got more and more excited. My husband and I decided we would wait until the day my period was due before testing, which was a Tuesday. So when I woke up on Monday, I sat down on the toilet and was shocked when I saw blood. I mean, jaw-dropping shocked. My mind went blank, and I literally did not know how to process what I was seeing.

For the past three weeks I was so focused on believing and standing on God's Word that I really was not expecting my period at all.

So I took a few moments and decided I did not believe it. I literally had to take a pregnancy test to confirm I was not pregnant, that this actually was my period, and that my mind and body were not playing tricks on me.

The pregnancy test revealed that I was not pregnant.

After the initial shock, I had to tell my husband we were not pregnant...again.

I really did not want to tell him. I wanted us to finally be able to celebrate. I wanted to feel all the excitement of planning how to tell our family and friends. I wanted to read about week-by-week growth of our baby and calculate a due date. I longed to talk about baby names, baby rooms, and every conversation that had been on hold because we were not there yet.

So, instead of all of those conversations, we had one we have had many times before. The problem with this one was, it hurt so much more. It hurt more because we stopped looking at the world, the science, the timing, and fears. Instead, we focused on God's Word, and we were confident he would answer our prayers.

When God did not answer our prayers, it felt like something was wrong. Was my faith not big enough? Were we being disobedient to God somewhere in our lives? Was there some unknown health issue we needed to pray against?

We were standing on God's Word, believing Mark 11:24: "Therefore I tell you, whatever you ask in prayer, believe that you have received it, and it will be yours." Still, the test was negative and my womb was empty. Another month of hope and another month of heartache.

As the years of painful disappointment flashed before my eyes, we realized we stood at a crossroads. We could choose to let this situation be for faith building or faith breaking.

We chose to let this build our faith because faith is about trusting our all-knowing and all-seeing God. Faith in God is having faith in the creator of our lives; it is trusting the God who speaks things into existence (Genesis 1:3, 1:6, 1:9, 1:11, 1:14,

1:20, 1:24, 1:26). If our faith breaks in him, then we really are hopeless.

Progressing forward from this heartache meant that we had to re-evaluate our situation. We continued to stand in faith, but we were challenged with not having the answers. We knew God was not the problem but did not know where the broken pieces were to try to fix them.

After praying through the brokenness, God revealed that having faith in him does not mean we have his knowledge. Isaiah 55:8 says, "For my thoughts are not your thoughts, neither are your ways my ways, declares the LORD." In this scripture, we are reminded that we do not have the big picture perspective God has. We cannot see all of the moving pieces and intricacies of his decision making and timing, and this is why we need to have faith while TTC.

When we know God can answer our prayers and he does not, it hurts. When a prayer is not answered, I know my broken heart asks, "Why?" But we have to find peace in knowing God has the answer, even if we do not. He has a reason we may never know, and if we truly trust God to answer this prayer, we can continue operating in faith no matter what the circumstances are.

If we lose our faith, we lose all of the promises he has given us in his Word. This month of hope turned to heartache, but we decided, instead of blaming God for the brokenness and pain, to look deeper, draw closer, and seek him further through obedience.

We can push God away or do the work through commitment and obedience and pull in as close as possible. The work we put into backing up our faith is what matters. If we do not do the work and choose to push God away, it only makes our faith useless. James 2:20 says, "Do you want to be shown, you foolish person, that faith apart from works is useless?"

The Bible also shows us, if we do not do the work, it makes our faith dead, shown in James 2:26: "For as the body apart from the spirit is dead, so also faith apart from works is dead." If we say we have faith, we have to live like we have faith so it is not dead and useless.

To live in faith, we can look to Jesus for our example, as it says in Hebrews 12:2–3: "looking to Jesus, the founder and perfecter of our faith, who for the joy that was set before him endured the cross, despising the shame, and is seated at the right hand of the throne of God. Consider him who endured from sinners such hostility against himself, so that you may not grow weary or fainthearted."

Jesus endured a challenge so much greater than we face so we may not grow weary. He is our example of faith and how to honor God. Because of Jesus, our sins are forgiven and we are reunited with God. His example of faith does not mean life will be easy. Jesus himself was even tempted by the enemy in Matthew 4, which reminds us that this is a battle.

Like Jesus, your faith will be challenged and hard days will come, but when we feel like we have been sucker punched spiritually and emotionally, it is time to turn to the Lord and trust him even more.

We can trust God with our brokenness because Psalm 34:18 shows us exactly where God is when we are hurting: "The LORD is near to the brokenhearted and saves the crushed in spirit."

When we are at our most broken, shattered selves, God is there. He is there, and he wants to get us through this pain and this heartache. He wants to comfort us and guide us, but we have to let him, which means we have to trust him.

I do not have a solid answer for why we did not get pregnant that month. Looking back, I know for certain God was not done growing me. God wanted more from me. He used this time to show me so much more that I did not even know I needed. I realize now that this was a crucial moment to continue trusting him and believing in his Word and in his abilities.

Thankfully, hope and faith in God will never let us down. We just have to trust him through all of the trials and not let our circumstances effect our faith.

REFLECTION AND PRAYER TIME
· ·

1. Where is your hope?

Are you tired of hoping because of the disappointment it brings?

Hope is not the enemy here, as I believed it was for a long time. The enemy is misplaced hope which leaves us more hopeless.

Prayerfully seek where to put your hope.

Romans 15:13, "May the God of hope fill you with all joy and peace in believing, so that by the power of the Holy Spirit you may abound in hope."

If your hope is in the Lord, you will find peace even in your heartache, even when things do not turn out the way you expect them to.

2. Peacefully wait on the Lord.

Philippians 4:6–7 says, "do not be anxious about anything, but in everything by prayer and supplication with thanksgiving let your requests be made known to God. And the peace of God, which surpasses all understanding, will guard your hearts and your minds in Christ Jesus."

The anxiety I had while waiting to find out if I was pregnant each month is evidence of lacking faith and patience.

When I finally was able to experience peace and trust while we were TTCTF, the anxiety was gone.

Waiting two weeks for an answer can seem like eternity, but you do not have to feel like your whole world is spinning out of control when you trust in the Lord. As you wait, use this time to draw even closer to God and to lean on him.

Two weeks are two weeks no matter how you look at it.

One thing I have found very helpful is to have a simple prayer that reminds me who is in control. My favorite is "God, I trust you with X." This could be trusting him with getting pregnant or with something else you find keeps coming up against your faith. It is simple and to the point, and you can say it a thousand times a day if you need to so you can keep giving this area over to God.

3. Will this build or break your faith?

Faith is powerful. Without faith, you will lose out on a lot of the promises God made in the Bible. I am not saying you cannot be frustrated or uncertain, but deal with those feelings so they do not interfere with your faith. Talk to your husband, and be honest about your emotions so your faith can grow.

When you are feeling like your faith is breaking, find at least one scripture to focus on for faith building, or do a Bible study based on faith building.

Remember, the Word is a lamp to your feet (Psalm 119:105); without it, you are wandering in darkness.

PRAYER

· · · · · · ·

God, my eyes are fixed on you, and I will no longer let my faith waver. My circumstances do not change you. My sin does not change you. You are the only constant in my life. You are the unmovable Rock. You are the unwavering King and my Holy God.

When my eyes see you for the glorious Father you are, I am certain nothing is impossible. I have let this time cloud my vision of you, and it has taken away my faith. It has made my faith weak and even useless.

Please forgive me for getting caught up in the details and forgetting how great you are. Please continue to renew my hope and strengthen my faith. Please rebuild this brokenness with a restored vision of your greatness.

There has been emptiness in my womb, but you, God, bring life. I will no longer let lack of faith betray the plans you have for me and rob me of your blessings. You take what is broken and make it whole.

Please, God, help me to conceive a baby this next cycle. Please help this baby to be healthy and strong. Please give our baby the best of our traits and pour out an abundance of your peace and joy in his or her life. Please allow this baby to grow to full term. Please bless me with an easy, pain-free delivery and quick recovery.

I rejoice in knowing you have heard this prayer and will answer it because my faith is no longer wavering and my hope and obedience are in you.

Thank you for remaining faithful, even in my unfaithfulness. I love you.

In Jesus' name,
Amen

Chapter 5

GETTING RIGHT WITH GOD

After getting through another month of heartache, I realized I could not sit around and wait anymore. I had been "waiting on God" for years, and nothing had changed. I know God does not need to change. I know God can bless us at any moment. Focusing our hope in God while TTCTF meant we had to continue growing in the Lord.

I was frustrated knowing God was capable of answering this prayer and chose not to. I knew he could bless us, but I was still not pregnant. Renewed in faith and standing on God's Word, I knew the only thing to do was to draw closer to him. I had to seek reasons why God was not answering my prayers.

One thing that became clear to me was that my lack of faith hurt my relationship with God. When we stop seeking God for decision making, leadership, and wisdom, we are saying he cannot handle these things. While this is not the intent of our actions, it is the message we are sending to our Creator.

Letting go of control might be hard, but how can we expect God to bless us when we do not follow his Word? It is important when TTCTF that we mend the damage we have done in the past through repentance.

Repentance is more than saying, "I'm sorry." It is acknowledging our sin as sin. It is asking and receiving forgiveness through the blood of Jesus (1 Peter 2:24) and completely changing our perspective to guard ourselves from continuing in sin and to avoid it completely.

Romans 12:2 says we are called to be transformed so we can have the discernment to determine God's will and not live in sin: "Do not be conformed to this world, but be transformed by the renewal of your mind, that by testing you may discern what is the will of God, what is good and acceptable and perfect."

When I realized I had become so self-reliant instead of God-reliant, I immediately had to change my perspective. I asked for forgiveness, repented, and determined to be transformed so I would receive a different outcome.

This was a big challenge because those fears kept coming back. It was hard work to change my thought process about the sin I had become used to living with. I had to renew my mind to let go of control and give it to the Lord.

I had to keep praying against my negative, controlling thoughts. As I did, my faith grew because I kept taking them to God. I kept reminding myself that he is enough and that if I trust him, I have to obey his Word.

Unfortunately, faith was not the only obstacle in the way of God blessing us with children. So while I kept working on faith, I also kept seeking God for what else I could do to get pregnant. I prayed daily, "Lord, I want to follow your will and glorify you. I ask that you guide my steps as I continue to draw closer to you..."

...and one day as I was praying, a person popped into my head: someone I had not talked to in years but was angry with. My initial thought was "I have to refocus on the prayer I am praying." But she kept coming up. She kept popping up in my head. I thought, "God, I do not understand. I am praying about this area of my life, not about that." In that moment I realized God cares about all areas of our lives, including the ones we tuck away and try to forget.

God revealed that if I wanted to follow his will, I had to do it in all areas of my life. I cannot be selective in my obedience. Sin is sin.

This world accepts sins like lying, cheating, stealing, having affairs, or even adulterous thoughts. The Bible clearly states that these are unacceptable to God.

Our relationship with God is just that—a relationship. We cannot hide the stuff we do not want to work on from God and distract him by saying, "Look what I'm doing over here—bless me." Even if we ask with all of the faith in the world, God has expectations of us, which he has made clear in his Word.

We have to honor God with our whole lives. This requires a deeper connection, not just prayers when we need something. We must give thanks for what we have. We need to seek him for instruction and wisdom. We need to be doers of God's Word so we can receive all that God has planned for us.

While I did not initially see the connection of disobedience, I am grateful God revealed this sin is relevant to what I was asking him for. He gave me this revelation, and I knew what I had to do.

Mark 11:25 says, "And whenever you stand praying, forgive, if you have anything against anyone, so that your Father also who is in heaven may forgive you your trespasses." So not only was eliminating this sin about obedience to his Word, this was about letting God accept my repentant heart. My "unrelated" sin now seemed very relevant.

I reached out to my old friend, asked for forgiveness for being angry, and was able to move forward in my walk with the Lord.

The situation with my friend was not something I thought of on a daily or even weekly basis, but it would pop up in my head and bother me. It was humbling to apologize, to admit I was hurt and reacted in anger. Thankfully, I had the ability to let go of my anger and move on. As soon as the conversation was over, I prayed and thanked God for revealing my sin.

Not a second later another friend popped into my head. I probably rolled my eyes. This was a lot of repentance in one day. I thought, "Okay, I won't fight this." I reached out to her as well.

Sometimes God calls us to be obedient in areas we do not even want to think about, but I think that is the nature of sin. We try to block it out and pretend like it is not there. But I was done letting sin stand in the way of God's blessings. I was trusting God to guide me, and when I reached out for his guidance, he gave it.

If we have faith in God to answer our prayers, we have to be open to his direction. It might even seem unrelated to our situation, but God's Word says in James 4:17, "So whoever knows the right thing to do and fails to do it, for him it is sin."

We cannot be in sin and expect God's blessings.

Jesus said in Luke 11:28, "Blessed rather are those who hear the word of God and keep it!" If we are seeking out the blessing of conception, we need to obey God's Word and his guidance, and we will be blessed.

We need to have God on our side. We already know we cannot do this alone. We see in 2 John 1:9 that we have work to do if we want God's help: "Everyone who goes on ahead and does not abide in the teaching of Christ, does not have God. Whoever abides in the teaching has both the Father and the Son." I see this scripture as an encouragement because to fully abide in the teachings of Jesus means there is always more work we can do. We are not living perfectly the way Jesus taught, which confirms we can keep working on our shortcomings and grow in our relationship with God. This solidifies that we will never have a reason to wait idly while hoping for one of God's promises.

I do not know where I would be today if I had ignored that nudge, if I had continued to ignore the answer God was giving. I am glad I was able to make the connection and see God was answering my prayers, just not in the way I was expecting. He heard me, and I was willing to obey, even though it was uncomfortable and humbling.

I was asking for guidance, and God was giving it. I was actively being obedient to God's calling in an effort to walk the path he planned for me, which I believed includes children.

Through this obedience, I was directly repairing my relationship with God. I was no longer being a hearer only of the Word but also a doer (James 1:22).

This is how we get right with God, and only good things come from repairing our relationship with our perfect Creator.

REFLECTION AND PRAYER TIME

. . . .

1. Are you relying on God?

Being self-reliant instead of God-reliant won't get us far in life. Even if everything in our past has taught us we can only rely on ourselves, that is not how God wants us to live.

Psalm 18:2 says, "The LORD is my rock and my fortress and my deliverer, my God, my rock, in whom I take refuge, my shield, and the horn of my salvation, my stronghold."

He has the strength we do not have and will guide us, direct us, and get us back on track. But we have to repent. Stop looking to the world for answers, and start looking to God and his Word.

Confess your sins to the Lord today. Ask for forgiveness and repent so you can be renewed in your thinking and repair your relationship with God.

2. Sin needs to be addressed.

We sin. We live in a sinful, lustful, prideful world. Ephesians 5:15–17 says, "Look carefully then how you walk, not as unwise but as wise, making the best use of the time, because the days are evil. Therefore do not be foolish, but understand what the will of the Lord is."

It is our responsibility to be on guard for sin and to try to eliminate it from our lives in these evil days.

1 Peter 2:8 says, "…They stumble because they disobey the Word…" If we stumble in sin, we can get back up through repenting and receiving forgiveness. If we do not repent but stay in our sin we will continue to stumble off of God's path and continue outside of his will.

3. We all have issues.

We all have areas in our lives we struggle with. You might not relate to needing to ask for forgiveness from a friend or family member, and that is okay. Please take this opportunity to pray for revelation of what sin you need to address in order to repair your relationship with God.

No matter what the sin is, God already knows and is ready to forgive you if you are ready to ask and obey his direction.

PRAYER

• • • • • • •

God, please do not let my sin stand in the way of your forgiveness and blessings.

Please show me how to honor you with my whole life, even if it means doing the hard work to get back on track.

I want to follow your will and glorify you. I want our relationship to be completely restored. Please forgive me, God, for everything that is outside of your will.

I ask that you guide my steps as I continue to draw closer to you. Help me to see the sin in my life so I can eliminate it.

I want to rely on you, Lord, not myself. I fall short, I do not have all the answers, and I often fail. You, God, are perfect and have a perfect plan already carved out for me. I want your perfect plan for my life.

Help me to hear your voice and obey your calling.

Mute the whispers of doubt and lies in my head so I can clearly hear your direction.

Help me to fully rely on you in this area and all areas of my life.

Thank you, God, for your clear direction so that in honoring you, I can be blessed with all your Word promises, including conception. I am so grateful for your faithfulness.

I love you.

In Jesus' name,
Amen

Chapter 6

UNITY IN MARRIAGE

Being a godly wife, as it says in Proverbs 31, has been a challenge for me. Through many years in my marriage I have found that I am an emotional person. These emotions affect my role as a wife. When I am angry or frustrated, it negatively impacts my marriage.

So when seven years passed by and we were not pregnant, it is safe to say I was frustrated. It was just one more frustration added to the already complex position of being a wife.

Within my frustrations, I did not honor God as the wife I had committed to be.

God revealed to me that I had to put aside my emotions and start working toward unity. I had to stop looking at how I felt when I responded and instead look to the Word for how I needed to act and react.

If we ignore the Word on our obligations in marriage, we are missing out on the many blessings God has for us. It is through obedience that we can stand on God's promises and receive all that he wants to bless us with, including children.

When we commit to each other in front of the world and God, we spiritually put our relationship in the cross-hairs of the enemy.

Matthew 19:6 says, "So they are no longer two but one flesh. What therefore God has joined together, let not man separate."

What God unifies, the devil wants to divide.

Thankfully, if there has been division, we can seek God for help and be unified again. No matter how great the division feels, God can repair and restore our marriages. Even if love fades and gets beat up along the way, the foundation of love comes from God, and through him it can be rebuilt.

By marital contract, we have chosen to be bound together, and the enemy does his best to separate us. He pins us against the very person who is, by God's definition, our other half. He takes our problems and makes them the focus in our marriage, weighing us down and pulling us apart.

This division in our marriage makes us incomplete. When divided, we do not magically become independent people; instead, we are split in half until we re-unify. To be complete, to be whole, we need to make sure our marriage does not have us divided in half.

We need to break the cycle of division the enemy is using to separate us. We need to stop letting our emotions negatively impact our marriages and start working on being godly wives.

I had to take responsibility for my part in our marriage and ensure I tried my best to honor God in my role as a wife.

I realized if I could love like it says in 1 Corinthians, then my emotions would not be able to cloud my judgment and cause division.

First Corinthians 13:4–8 (NIV) says, "Love is patient, love is kind. It does not envy, it does not boast, it is not proud. It does not dishonor others, it is not self-seeking, it is not easily angered, it keeps no record of wrongs. Love does not delight in evil but rejoices with the truth. It always protects, always trusts, always hopes, always perseveres. Love never fails…"

Love. Never. Fails.

Emotions cloud our judgment and effect the way we show love. They shut us down from rational thinking and allow this wave of uncontrolled frustrations to take over. Emotions are capable of manipulating our thought process and separating us even further. They distract us from what God really wants from us: to serve him according to his Word. This emotional kind of reaction is not the biblical love the Bible talks about.

Biblically, love takes work. This work is clearly defined, and it is not all easy. If we work on all of the traits that represent biblical love in our marriage, it becomes hard to be divided.

Biblical Love

- Is patient *Be more patient*
- Is kind *Be Kind*
- Is not envious *Don not be envious*
- Is not boastful *Do not boast*
- Is not proud *Do not be too proud*
- Honors each other
- Is not selfish *Do not be Selfish*
- Is slow to anger *Do not be Angry*
- Keeps no record of wrongs
- Rejects evil *Reject Evil, Enemy*
- Rejoices with truth *Be Honest*
- Protects each other
- Trusts each other *Trust others*
- Hopes *Be Hopeful*
- Perseveres

If we have all of these traits in our marriages, love will never fail.

When one trait is lacking, we are not fully loving each other. Applying all of these pieces to our marriages takes work, and it is unending work.

We made the covenant to love one another all the days of our lives in front of God and the world. It is our job to make sure that we are loving each other the way the Bible explains love.

It is only through this kind of love that we can fully honor God through our roles as husband and wife and receive his blessings.

Biblical Role of the Husband

Ephesians 5:25–29 says, "Husbands, love your wives, as Christ loved the church and gave himself up for her, that he might sanctify her, having cleansed her by the washing of water with the word, so that he might present the church to himself in splendor, without spot or wrinkle or any such thing, that she might be holy and without blemish. In the same way husbands should love their wives as their own bodies. He who loves his wife loves himself. For no one ever hated his own flesh, but nourishes and cherishes it, just as Christ does the church."

First Peter 3:7 says, "Likewise, husbands, live with your wives in an understanding way, showing honor to the woman as the weaker vessel, since they are heirs with you of the grace of life, so that your prayers may not be hindered."

Biblical Role of the Wife

First Corinthians 11:3 tells us, "But I want you to understand that the head of every man is Christ, the head of a wife is her husband, and the head of Christ is God."

Ephesians 5:22–24 says, "Wives, submit to your own husbands, as to the Lord. For the husband is the head of the wife even as Christ is the head of the church, his body, and is himself its Savior. Now as the church submits to Christ, so also wives should submit in everything to their husbands."

Additionally, the role of a godly wife is to be a helper. Genesis 2:18 says, "Then the LORD God said, 'It is not good that the man should be alone; I will make him a helper fit for him.'"

We were created to be an important support for our husbands, which is also confirmed in 1 Corinthians 11:8–9: "For a man was not made from woman, but woman from man. Neither was man created for woman, but woman for man."

Our job as a wife is to help.

Honoring God in Our Roles

We have to be obedient to God's Word. The Bible specifically says if we hear the word and do not act on what we know to be true, we are only deceiving ourselves, found in James 1:19–22: "Know this, my beloved brothers: let every person be quick to hear, slow to speak, slow to anger; for the anger of man does not produce the righteousness of God. Therefore put away all filthiness and rampant wickedness and receive with meekness the implanted word, which is able to save your souls. But be doers of the word, and not hearers only, deceiving yourselves."

When obedience to God's Word gets difficult, we have to remember that God designed us. It is through pride and pain that we decide our ways are better than his. God knows what works best in our marriages, and he wants us to be unified. God is our Father, our Creator, and he does not wish us harm.

Instead of continuing in a broken marriage, we need to unify our marriages. Without unity, there is division. Since division does not come from the Lord, it is safe to say we are acting outside of his will. It should not be surprising when our prayers are not being answered when we have this division. We need to resolve the problems so we are honoring God.

If your marriage is suffering, God can restore it through obedience and prayer. Through our obedience, God will bless us.

Marriage can be filled with joy and support, compassion, love, and respect. It can be everything God intended. In order to get there, work has to be done. Even if we feel hopeless, our hope can be renewed because the Lord has plans to prosper and not harm us. Jeremiah 29:11 (NIV) says, "'For I know the plans I have for you,' declares the LORD, 'plans to prosper you and not to harm you, plans to give you hope and a future.'"

God designed this unification in our marriages. He needs our obedience here just as much as he requires it everywhere else in our lives. Having a united marriage is honoring God because, like it says in Matthew 19:6, God has joined you together.

If we honor God's Word, we will actively draw nearer to him. In return, he promises to draw near to us (James 4:8). With God drawing near, we receive a clearer understanding of his will for our lives and can eliminate the reasons why God is waiting to answer our prayers.

When I let my emotions cloud my perspective, I am setting up my marriage for a fight. While I know emotions are always going to be there, they cannot take away from the biblical love I give to my husband. I have had to make a conscious effort to express those emotions with biblical love, so that I am not dividing my marriage.

When I love consistently, my marriage is protected because I am reacting the way God expects me to, no matter what I feel emotionally. Through reacting in love, our marriage stays unified even if there is an argument. When our marriage is unified, there is peace and joy in our house, and it is one more area in which we are honoring God.

This has not been easy. Ultimately, we both had to surrender, eliminate the pride, and work on loving each other the way God intended us to. Having a marriage filled with God's love is worth surrendering and obeying to God and his direction.

REFLECTION AND PRAYER TIME

. . . .

1. Honoring God In Your Role

Ephesians 5:33 says, "However, let each one of you love his wife as himself, and let the wife see that she respects her husband."

Reflect on your roles as husband and wife. Take responsibility for your actions, and change them to honor God. Even imperfect effort is better than continuing to disobey God's Word.

There is a lot more in the Bible about marriage. Find a Bible study or a book on Christian marriage to help strengthen this area of your life.

Scriptures to read and pray about are 1 Peter 3:1–2, Ephesians 5:22–24, 1 Corinthians 11:7–9, and 1 Corinthians 11:3.

God will bless your obedience and will strengthen your marriage as you honor his Word.

2. Prayer

Prayer is where we can petition God for help, healing, and hope. Prayer is where we get the strength from God when we just do not have any left. Prayer is how we re-unify and fight this spiritual battle to overcome division. Keep praying for your marriage, together and apart.

3. The Benefits of a Loving Marriage

While this effort is to honor God and his Word, it also makes your marriage a happier place, with less fighting, more communicating, more joy, and more love. God will honor this commitment and will draw nearer to you.

When we are united in Christ, God is able to work through us as married couples and bless us even more.

PRAYER

· · · · · · ·

God, I know division does not come from you. I know you are the unifying bond that holds my marriage together. Through the good times and the bad times, you are the constant that guides us.

Through marriage, I have tied my heart and life to my husband, and the enemy continues to challenge me on this commitment. He tries to add bitterness, resentment, and anger. He tries to strip out love and replace it with his evil ways.

There is no place in my marriage for the king of division. I will no longer be deceived by the serpent. I will look to your Word for guidance, and I will seek your love for direction. I will set my heart on being a biblical wife. I will not let my emotions cloud my commitment that I made to my husband and to you, God.

I will serve you as his wife. I will serve him as his wife. I will honor you even when it is easier not to, because anything else is serving the enemy. Anything else let's the devil into our commitment. Anything else separates us from your unifying power.

Thank you for giving such clear instruction for my role as a wife in your Word.

Please help me to honor you.

Please help me to seek you in my marriage.

Please take this brokenness and use it to bring you glory.

Please let our unity produce fruit more precious than I could ever imagine. Thank you, Lord.

In Jesus' name,
Amen

Chapter 7

HONORING THE BODY

Honoring God in this broken body required a major reset in the way I thought about myself. This body was not working the way I wanted it to.

I was so frustrated because I felt like any effort I put into being healthier did not matter. I still was not pregnant. But the Bible says to glorify God in our bodies in 1 Corinthians 6:19–20: "Or do you not know that your body is a temple of the Holy Spirit within you, whom you have from God? You are not your own, for you were bought with a price. So glorify God in your body."

This scripture is hard because we look at our bodies as our own, as the flawed broken remnants of what God had originally designed. We have picked them apart and studied them. We have wished and prayed for them to change, and they have disappointed us over and over again by their imperfections.

We now are faced with the fact that our bodies are supposed to be temples. That they are actually not our own and because of the price that was paid, we are required to glorify God even in the brokenness of our bodies.

Accepting this command, I decided I wanted to honor God with my body by taking better care of it. It was clear this was another part of my disobedience to the Lord. I believe this was another reason God had to wait for me to recognize my sin and repent before blessing us with a child.

God gifted us with one body and the ability to care for it properly.

I was inconsistent.

I was resentful.

I was failing.

Now I had the opportunity to take care of my body by honoring God consistently instead of only during the two weeks I thought I was pregnant each month.

This perspective gave me endurance that I never had before. It allowed me to focus on better health choices without focusing on my circumstances. This process continued to remind me that I am not in control and that I am not alone. God is here and is willing to guide us. The body I had resented for so long was now being treated as the gift that it truly was.

What I do each day to this gift is either honoring God with my choices or defiling his temple that houses the Holy Spirit.

These bodies are not perfect, but they are what we have. They are what God gave us, and the obstacles we face in them will only be harder if we resent them. If we embrace this gift and are grateful for what we have, it will be easier to honor them and obey God's Word.

Our bodies were designed by God to do great things, and there is no health issue that is too big for God to overcome. But we need to overcome the obstacles in our lives that are outside of his will because God wants our obedience. John 14:15 (NIV) says, "If you love me, keep my commands."

We have to honor what God has blessed us with, even in conditions that are not what we hope for.

God gave us one body, which he designed perfectly. Psalm 100:3 says, "Know that the LORD, he is God! It is he who made us, and we are his; we are his people, and the sheep of his pasture."

God made us perfectly. Unfortunately, because we are born into sin, we lose that perfection. Some of us lose it before we are born, while the rest of us lose our perfect health as we live in this imperfect world. However, that is not an excuse to take shortcuts and ignore our bodies' needs.

So if getting pregnant is an equation, part of the equation has to include honoring the bodies God gave us. They are the vessels we need to grow our babies in, and even if they are not perfect, we have to treat these vessels with respect.

That respect requires us to make the adjustments necessary to be well and prepare the home for our child. There are even recommendations specifically for conception to adjust our diets found in the Bible. In Judges chapter 13 we learn about a man named Manoah who's wife was barren. An angel appeared to her and told her she would conceive a child and he gave her these instructions in Judges 13:4, "Therefore be careful and drink no wine or strong drink, and eat nothing unclean..."

For me, I knew what needed to be done to be healthy. My diet needed to change, and I needed to be consistent without letting my negative urine tests get the better of me for two weeks each month.

I found doing a whole body cleanse to be a great body reset tool. Two I do regularly can be found at ttctf.com/resources. A detox can help jump-start your health in the right direction. Detoxing is also something you cannot do once you become pregnant, so now is the best time to try to eliminate toxic buildup from your body.

After a full-body cleanse, it is important to keep processed foods, which negatively affect our health, out of the diet. I highly recommend following the Whole30 diet. It is a thirty-day commitment, and there are a lot of resources online for support. While it is a thirty-day diet, this often turns into lifestyle changes for people because of how good they feel in such a short amount of time.

If you choose to focus on eliminating foods that negatively affect your health without following a specific protocol, below is a great starting point of foods to research concerning the negative impacts they have on our health.

- Caffeine (decaf and regular)
- Dairy
- Fast food
- Highly processed foods
- Soda
- White flour
- GMO foods
- Soy
- Produce with high amounts of pesticides
- Man-made sweeteners, processed sugar

None of these foods are beneficial to our health; in fact, they can be very harmful. They can cause all sorts of health ailments and make it harder to get pregnant, stay pregnant, and grow a healthy baby. These foods can also make it challenging to breastfeed.

We have one body, and it is time to put the effort in to make sure it is getting the right fuel to function properly, the way God designed it.

First Corinthians 10:31 says, "So, whether you eat or drink, or whatever you do, do all to the glory of God." Even what we eat and drink needs to be for the glory of God. I know this is a challenge, but it is worth it.

As I have prayed to get pregnant while TTCTF, I have to remind myself as I am shouting to God in frustration, begging for blessings, that I cannot ignore the ones he has already given.

Why would we expect to receive anything more if we do not honor God today with the abundance he has given us?

Thankfully God forgives us and can help us in all of the things we struggle with.

This may be a very hard part of your equation, but without addressing the health and care of our bodies, we are missing out on a major opportunity to glorify and obey God.

For me, the desire in my heart to have children was so much greater than overcoming any obstacle that stood in the way of God's blessings.

REFLECTION AND PRAYER TIME

1. Honor what God has given you.

This may be with your body, your house, your car, or your time.

Prayerfully reflect on all you have been given and know it does not have to be perfect to be a blessing. Your car might be close to dying, but today it is a blessing. Your house might need a new roof, but today it is a blessing. Your body might have something holding you back from getting pregnant, but today it is a blessing because you are alive.

Today is a gift that most will take for granted, but God gave you today; not everyone will get this gift.

2. Take action.

When we recognize sin, we need to take action. Pray for revelation and help with repentance so we can make improvements.

If your health is suffering, make a change today. Do not wait any longer. Forget about perfection, and just do better today than you did yesterday.

Take a step in the right direction. Ask God to light a path at your feet and take the steps one at a time. I know he will honor your obedience and help you along the way.

PRAYER

• • • • • • •

God, I know this body is a gift, and I know I take it for granted. I know with all of its faults, it still has strengths. I know that as awesome as it is, I resent it for not being more.

But today God, I realize that if I want more from this body, I have to love it. I have to take care of it. I have to honor it as the temple of your Holy Spirit.

I have tried many times, I have promised many times, and I have failed just as many.

Today God, please help me change. Please help me see this body the way you see it. Please help me have the strength and the desire to honor this gift. I literally cannot do this without you.

This world has taught me that I am not enough if I am not perfect, but you, God, accept me in my flaws and you shine in them. You take hold of my weaknesses and use them for your glory.

You are so good, God, that you can take something so broken and put it back together better than it ever was before.

Please restore this body and this mind. Please strengthen me to honor you by being diligent in taking care of this blessing. Every breath I breathe is by your design, your creation, and your purpose. Help me to see that goodness in myself; help me to not be deceived by the illusion of perfection, and to help me be encouraged by the work you have planned for me in this body.

Thank you for being my strength in this weakness. I love you, Lord.

In Jesus' name,
Amen

Chapter 8

GOD'S PLAN

Jeremiah 29:11–13 states, "For I know the plans I have for you, declares the LORD, plans for welfare and not for evil, to give you a future and a hope. Then you will call upon me and come and pray to me, and I will hear you. You will seek me and find me, when you seek me with all your heart."

God has a plan for you and your life. This plan is good.

Our plans fail and fall short. I have learned this after many failed plans. Having tried for seven years to get pregnant without faith has proven unfruitful.

Without seeking God with all of our hearts, we will not find Him (v. 13). This choice leaves us alone in our plans and living without God's direction, guidance, and blessings.

We have to trust that whatever his plan is, even if it is different than ours, it is better. His plans will be more fulfilling, joyful, and fruitful. Surrendering our plans and following God's is what trust looks like.

So without being a total downer, it is time to ask this question: Has God told you no?

I understand what this question means and know that it is probably scary. This is where trust has to come in or our faith will break. God sometimes says no to prayers, but he does so with a purpose. Before we continue, I want to be clear that "no" is the exception, not the rule when we look in the Bible. Time and time again, the Bible shows us that through faith, God answers our prayers.

This question is something I struggled with. After years and years of negative tests and a boatload of fears, I started to wonder if God was telling me no. I even shifted my plans to have a childless life. Then God renewed my hope and faith through revelation. During our first month of TTCTF, I was bummed I did not get pregnant right away. Then, after the second month of TTCTF, it hurt more, and with that pain came an important question: "How do we know this is God's plan for our lives?"

We understood unanswered prayers from God does not mean his answer is no. But now we were putting in the work and still not receiving this promise. So this question tripped me up for a few days. I did not have an answer. The Bible says we can have children, so questioning this seems counterintuitive, but it is a question my husband and I had to face.

Trusting in God, we turned to him. We reflected, prayed, and read in the Bible about a time when a prayer was not answered.

Paul had been suffering with a thorn in his flesh in 2 Corinthians 12:8–9, and he brought his suffering to God: "Three times I pleaded with the Lord about this, that it should leave me. But he said to me, 'My grace is sufficient for you, for my power is made perfect in weakness.'"

In this scripture we had our answer. God wanted Paul to have this thorn. It had a purpose for God's glory. Our revelation came because God specifically told Paul no. Paul had pursued God for healing, and he did not get an answer right away. After continuing to ask God for healing, God answered and made it clear he was not going to remove this thorn.

Paul was not asking God if this was his will, nor was he doubting God's abilities. Paul continued asking God for this healing because he was certain God could deliver it.

Even though this was not the answer Paul wanted to hear, Paul trusted God in the plan for his life. We see this in Paul's response to God in 2 Corinthians 12:10, which says, "For the sake of Christ, then, I am content with weaknesses, insults, hardships, persecutions, and calamities. For when I am weak, then I am strong."

Paul trusted God even when the answer was no. We have to trust God even when the answer is no. But let's be clear, unless God tells us no, we cannot doubt. We have to stand on his Word and his promises and believe he will answer our prayers.

We have to keep pursuing him and know that if this is not God's plan, he will tell us no. Everything else in the Bible points to the answer being yes. We need to trust that God can answer this prayer and be unrelenting in our pursuit of receiving this gift.

In Matthew chapter 15:21–28 we see a Canaanite woman who pursued Jesus relentlessly until he answered her prayer. When she asked Jesus to heal her daughter, Jesus was silent. He literally said nothing to her. As she continued, the disciples did not want her to make a scene, so they asked Jesus to send her away. So, Jesus said to her, "I was sent only to the lost sheep of the house of Israel." This woman did not walk away or give up, this woman had great faith because she continued to ask him for help. They go back and forth another round. Jesus responded in Matthew 15:28, "'O woman, great is your faith! Be it done for you as you desire.' And her daughter was healed instantly."

This woman faced silence, pleading her case to Jesus without relenting so her prayer would be answered. She did this because she knew he was worth pursuing. It did not matter that he initially did not speak to her. It did not matter when he finally spoke to her, it was not what she wanted to hear. Her pursuit did not stop until her request was answered.

Our doubt can make us stop pursuing him before we receive the blessings he has for us. However, if we have unrelenting faith and believe the countless promises which are fulfilled in God's Word, we would not stop pursuing him until we received this gift. Mark 11:23 says, "Truly, I say to you, whoever says to this mountain, 'Be taken up and thrown into the sea,' and does not doubt in his heart, but believes that what he says will come to pass, it will be done for him."

Doubting makes the mountain unmovable. Doubting makes our prayers unanswered. The question to determine if God will or won't answer our prayers is designed to cause doubt, and we all face it at some point. It is designed to break us and hurt us and take away the blessings God has for us. We need to be certain of the answer to this question.

The answer is yes unless God tells you specifically no.

The enemy will use your past experiences to convince you that you will never get pregnant. He is a liar. He will keep inserting questions designed to make you doubt.

If you take these questions to God, search his Word, and trust in him, the enemy will not be able to plant seeds of doubt in your heart. This keeps us on guard from being manipulated to believe God is saying something he has not actually said. This allows us to focus on God when we normally would doubt and waver. This allows us to be free in receiving all that God has planned for us.

Without doubting, and having complete faith and trust in him, we are pleasing God, and the Bible says in 1 John 3:22, "and whatever we ask we receive from him, because we keep his commandments and do what pleases him." If we set our hearts to please God, whatever we ask he will give it.

God has a reason for his timing. If we are trusting God's plan for our lives, we can be unrelenting in pursuing him for this blessing.

We can trust that if he has not answered this prayer yet, there is a reason. We can use this time to seek out his will and follow his commands so our lives align with his plan, and through our commitment to him, we will find ourselves back in his will; that is when we truly are blessed.

REFLECTION AND PRAYER TIME

• •

1. Eliminating The Doubt of No

If God has not told you no, then do not accept no as an answer. Only God has the power and authority to tell you no. Anything else is a lie. Look at the promises in the Word, and stand on them in the authority of Jesus Christ our Savior.

2. Trusting His Plan

Do you fully trust God and his plan for your life?

No matter what obstacles you are facing, he is prepared. He has an answer, and he has a plan. He has the foresight we will never have. He is our loving father who knows us better than we know ourselves.

Can you afford not to trust God fully in the plans for your life?

3. Waiting on God's Plan

When we are forced to wait, it is a challenge to our faith and hope.

When we lack patience while we wait, it breeds frustration, which starts a cycle that robs us of the blessings God has promised in his Word.

Remember, you do not have to be idle in your waiting. You should be actively seeking him and working on growth. This will bring fruit to your waiting, and you may even find your patience strengthening and your trust growing.

PRAYER

· · · · · · ·

God, I trust your plans for my life. I trust they are for good and not for harm. Time has passed by, and my plans have failed. I know if I do not make a change, they will continue to fail. I know, God, if I can surrender this broken heart, you can heal it completely.

Please help me surrender my plans.

Show me where to step, and I will step there. Show me where I am not obeying, and I will correct it.

Please make my will line up with your will. Make my plans your plans.

Please reveal to me when the questions in my mind and heart are causing doubt so I can eliminate all forms of doubt.

I trust in you and your timing. I trust that you are the answer to my prayers. I trust that your answer is "yes" because you have not told me "no."

I will seek you with my whole heart. I will know your Word and I will know your ways so I can be guarded against sin. I will rejoice in the waiting, in your timing, and in the testimony this journey will produce.

I will see mountains move in your name, and my faith will continue to grow. I believe you will answer this prayer, open my womb, and gift me with a healthy conceived child.

Thank you, God, for revelation and for answers to questions. I love you.

In Jesus' name,
Amen

Chapter 9

FIGHTING DECEPTION

The devil is a deceiver. He asked one question that was enough to change the course of our existence.

Genesis 3:1 (NIV) says, "Now the serpent was more crafty than any of the wild animals the Lord God had made. He said to the woman, 'Did God really say, "You must not eat from any tree in the garden?"'"

As you may remember, a tiny bit of doubt was all it took for Eve to be deceived. Deception creeps in; it is sneaky and crafty. It causes enough doubt for us to question God.

Thoughts like "God doesn't love me" or "God doesn't care about me." Or more subtle thoughts that lower our self-esteem and make us feel unworthy to have God's blessings, are all tools of the deceiver.

These thoughts affect our walk with God, they affect our trust in him, and they cause division between us and God. These thoughts, if believed, can keep us from the very blessings God's Word promises us.

These thoughts make us doubt God.

Instead of having doubt, we need to follow 2 Corinthians 10:5 (NIV), which says, "We demolish arguments and every pretension that sets itself up against the knowledge of God, and we take captive every thought to make it obedient to Christ."

We need to take every thought captive and make it obedient to Christ. That is pretty intense instruction. But if we really can take our negative thoughts or lies and make them obedient to Christ, we would be even closer to God.

We need to be able to recognize the deception and, instead of believing it, call it out for the lie that it is. We can only recognize these lies if we are on guard for them and are living in truth. If we have the Word in our hearts, discerning truth becomes a much faster process.

What makes us choose to believe anything? We take a piece of information and question it and think about it, and ultimately the research we have done on that question gets us to believe it or not. Our research can be a long process or a very short one depending on the amount of effort we put in. If the source is our own thoughts and our own doubts, there is a much higher probability we will believe it without doing more research, even if it is not true.

The lies we believe affect our relationship with God. When our relationship with God is filled with doubt and uncertainty, God cannot bless us the way his Word has promised. All of the promises in God's Word come with instructions on how to receive them. We have to trust, we have to eliminate doubt, and we have to have faith.

God knows when we do not follow these biblical instructions. He is all-knowing and all-seeing. We cannot hide our thoughts from Him. Psalm 69:5 says, "O God, you know my folly; the wrongs I have done are not hidden from You."

This is why we have to take all of our thoughts captive, line them up with the Bible, and pray about them. This is the only way we can find and face the lies and trust in God without doubting in order to receive the blessing of conception.

James 1:6–8 says doubt actually makes us unstable: "But let him ask in faith, with no doubting, for the one who doubts is like a wave of the sea that is driven and tossed by the wind. For that person must not suppose that he will receive anything from the Lord; he is a double-minded man, unstable in all his ways."

To stand on the promises his Word has for us, like getting pregnant, we need to make sure we are not vulnerable to the craftiness of the enemy. We need to be stable in our faith. Any doubt needs to be crushed or we won't receive anything from the Lord, as it says in James 1:7.

We need to take inventory of our thoughts and beliefs and make sure they line up with the Word of God. I know this is easier said than done, but we are accountable for our thoughts. We do not want to believe lies and cause division between us and God.

When we find an area in which we have been deceived, we need to repent and pray against those lies. We get to find freedom in Jesus because we are forgiven, and then our relationship with God is restored.

Once a lie has been revealed, it is important to find the root of that lie. Is it from a person, something you read, or a memory from your childhood? The source of the lie should be addressed to prevent it from sneaking back in.

Deception is a perversion of the truth. God does not want us to be deceived. He will guard and protect us from deception because he is faithful, as it says in 2 Thessalonians 3:3: "But the Lord is faithful. He will establish you and guard you against the evil one."

One area I have struggled with is being a perfectionist. I wanted to be a perfect mom. Knowing that I could not be perfect meant I would fail as a mom. This meant before I even got pregnant, I was failing.

This unattainable goal that God does not even expect from me robbed me over and over again. It was not until God revealed that he is prepared for my imperfections that I stopped being deceived by unattainable goals. He is prepared for my flaws, and he fills in the broken pieces. In my imperfections, I will still be able to be the mom God needs me to be because I am trusting him to help with my shortcomings.

Using our past and our thoughts against us is the crafty work of the enemy. My thoughts should not be used against me, but until I trusted God with them, they were. Over and over, our conscious and subconscious minds deceive us; the originator of our deception could be the devil himself or our own self doubt. Either way, if we believe these lies, we are being manipulated and we are the ones who are missing out.

Being aware of the negative thought patterns we have allows us to see what the devil may use to manipulate us. When the truth is revealed, we stop being confused by thoughts that do not line up with God's Word.

In chapter two, I revealed I had fear about having children because I felt alone. Through counseling, I realized that God was always by my side and will help me through raising children. I was never alone and would never be alone.

If I did not have that revelation, I would not have replaced my fear with trusting in God. If I had not trusted God to get us pregnant, I know it never would have happened.

As I searched for reasons why I was an easy target for manipulation and deception, I found the root of my fear was based on my childhood memories and the way my brain interpreted specific situations.

Many lies get planted in our childhood because we do not understand how to process negative experiences properly. Experiencing something that made us feel alone, unworthy, or any other negative feelings, can spill into our relationship with God.

These feelings can become underlying beliefs we hold onto in our walk with God and can affect our perspective and decision making.

Thankfully we can pray and seek the Word for truth. We also have the opportunity to reprocess those negative memories so they no longer deceive us.

EMDR (Eye Movement Desensitization and Reprocessing) is a scientific way to revisit memories so they can be reprocessed and re-filed properly to stop them from negatively affecting us.

Using this technique has been a blessing for me. This therapy helped reveal where my negative thoughts originated. When I was able to properly process those thoughts, the deceiver could no longer manipulate my thought process to drive a wedge between me and God.

EMDR revealed to me why I felt and thought the way I did. It gave me the opportunity to correct my thought patterns, so I would no longer be misled by my past. This stopped the lies from interfering with my relationship with God.

EMDR, coupled with prayer, reading the Bible, and searching our hearts for truth, is an excellent defense against deception.

It can be humbling to admit we have been deceived. I certainly justified my fears as rational, but when I held them up to God's Word, they were wrong. Humility is rewarded in our walk with God.

Psalm 25:8–9 says, "Good and upright is the LORD; therefore he instructs sinners in the way. He leads the humble in what is right, and teaches the humble his way."

Showing up and putting the effort in even though we have been wrong before is evidence of trusting in God. Letting God lead us will ensure we are no longer being deceived.

When deception is eliminated, all that is left is truth, which fills us with peace and hope. Let's get the lies out of our heads and enjoy the truth reigning in our lives and our hearts.

REFLECTION AND PRAYER TIME

1. Revelation of Deception

Ask God to reveal lies that have deceived you, and replace them with truth.

Our God is truth. There is no deception with him.

What we believe is our choice. We can choose to seek out truth or believe lies.

If we put pride aside, we can find peace in knowing we serve a perfect God who can help us, even through deception.

2. Building Your Defense

Pray.

Read the Bible.

Search out a Christian EMDR specialist at www.EMDR.com. Commit to a few sessions.

You can discuss things you are aware of or talk about your current situation and frustrations. From there, you will be guided through an EMDR session and will know within a few sessions if it is helping.

PRAYER

· · · · · · ·

God, I see the story of Eve, and the deception breaks my heart. She let one question cloud her trust in you, which changed the course of our lives today. That deception allowed sin to enter this world. Now here I stand before you, God, with doubts of my own. I am so sorry, God. I do not want my doubts to distort my trust in you. I do not want to question your promises, your Word, or your abilities.

I want to be stable in my walk with you.

If I continue in doubt, I see that I may not be able to receive this gift of conception. I see that doubt holds back blessings; it interferes with our relationship and even causes sin. I will eliminate the doubt in my life, God. I will stop listening to anything that is against your Word. If I have questions, I will go to your Word to look for answers.

I will not listen to lies.

I will no longer think or speak lies.

I will no longer be an easy target for manipulation by the enemy.

Please help me take captive every thought and make it obedient to you.

Thank you, God, for helping me to see through the deception. Thank you for turning this doubt into faith in you. Thank you, God, for allowing me to grow in you and ultimately for allowing me to conceive a child.

I am so grateful for your forgiveness. Thank you, God.

In Jesus' name,
Amen

Chapter 10

TRUSTING GOD

Romans 12:12 says, "Rejoice in hope, be patient in tribulation, be constant in prayer."

I clearly did not have Romans 12:12 on my heart as seven years of waiting were unfruitful in our desire to become pregnant. I hated hope; it felt meaningless. I was not patient when each month passed, and unfortunately, I was not constant in prayer.

My frustration with not getting pregnant turned me against the traits God expected of me, which are clearly written out in his Word. Not following Romans 12:12 was evidence that I was not trusting God. If I ever expected to get pregnant, I had to learn how to trust God again, and if I was able to follow Romans 12:12, I would prove to myself and God that I did trust him.

I had to learn how to be hopeful and patient and how to become relentless in praying even when I did not receive what I was asking God for. These became my goals and milestones to track my trust in God because they were so far from how I had previously tried to conceive.

Previously I was frustrated, trying to force an outcome that I was unable to produce. If I was going to petition God to hear and answer my prayers, I needed to come to him with complete trust.

On paper, it sounds easy to trust God. He created us and knows everything there is to know about us. He speaks and life is formed. There is nothing outside of his reach. But our frustration, anger, resentment, and impatience are not the fruit of trusting our Creator. These traits leave us fruitless and void of the characteristics God expects of his children. These traits prove that we do not trust God.

I can tell you from experience, if we do not fully trust God, we will continue to be fruitless—fruitless in our prayers, in our efforts, and in our wombs.

The amazing thing is we can trust God without being frustrated or angry, not just because he is our God but because he specifically wants us to be able to have children. The Bible says children are a reward from God in Psalm 127:3, which states, "Behold, children are a heritage from the LORD, the fruit of the womb a reward."

Rewards are something we earn. This entire book is about seeking out the will of God, being obedient to what we find, and in turn having faith and trust that God will reward our efforts.

The enemy does not want us to receive any reward from God and will use anything he can to drive a wedge between us and our Heavenly Father. John 10:10 says, "The thief comes only to steal and kill and destroy. I came that they may have life and have it abundantly."

Our God gives abundant life, and the enemy has come to steal from us, including the blessings of children. We need to overcome our frustrations by learning to trust God and his timing with patience while pursuing him for this blessing.

Patient in Tribulation

If we completely trust God, we will have patience while we wait to get pregnant, as we are called to do in Romans 12:12. Right now, this is a time of waiting in hopes of conceiving a baby. There are many scriptures about waiting that give us more instructions during this season in our lives.

Psalm 27:14 says, "Wait for the LORD; be strong, and let your heart take courage; wait for the LORD!"

Psalm 130:5–6 says, "I wait for the LORD, my soul waits, and in his word I hope; my soul waits for the LORD more than watchmen for the morning, more than watchmen for the morning."

In both of these verses we see that we need to wait, but there are more instructions we need to follow for us to fully obey these scriptures. They say to be strong, take courage, and hope, which all require our trust in God. If we choose to wait without the rest of these attributes, we are not fully following God's Word. We are taking a portion of it and applying it to our lives without looking at the remaining context.

If we do not continue with the rest of what God calls us to do, we will find ourselves missing out on his blessings.

I found myself saying many times while TTC, "We are just waiting on the Lord. It will happen in his timing." And it was true, but that was all I was doing. I started using this statement as a crutch, as a reason for God to hold onto the blessings his Word promised us. As I leaned on those statements, I grew resentful and bitter because I knew God could bless us at any time but did not.

These frustrations became my focus, and I stopped pursuing the Lord the way I biblically should have. This is when I realized I was not being patient during this tribulation. Instead I was frustrated because of how long it was taking for God to answer my prayers. What I did not realize in my frustration was that God was actually waiting on me.

This is why seven years of waiting were unfruitful. God was waiting for my faith and trust to grow, but instead, it was shrinking because I stopped seeking him. I started to believe the lie that God was not answering my prayers because he did not love me or want to bless me.

I finally set aside my frustrations and realized God wants more from me than just waiting. He wants action. He wants our hearts. He wants our commitment. Until we are ready to take responsibility for what we are doing wrong, God will continue to wait on us until we get the message.

After God revealed what I needed to surrender in order to trust him, the frustration, bitterness, and resentment left me. They were replaced with joy, genuine hope, and confidence in God's timing. This gave us peace and patience as we waited for our baby.

Constant in Prayer

So much of TTCTF is about our relationship with God. Without the revelations God gave me through prayer and reading the Bible, I would never have gone beyond my own presumptions. I would not have seen things the way God needed me to.

Prayer is how we communicate with God. It does not have to be eloquent, forced, or proper. It just has to happen.

I remember in my youth group the question came up about the proper way to pray. I suggested we not pray to God while on the toilet, and my youth pastor asked me, "Why not?"

He challenged me just by asking why, and I could not come up with a good enough reason not to.

My initial thought was that it was not respectful or appropriate to pray on the toilet. We are supposed to be respectful of God, but talking to God, praying to him, asking him for guidance in everything is what being constant in prayer is about. If we are sitting on the toilet and need God, there is no reason not to reach out to him.

Because we can pray to God on the toilet, we also need to accept that we do not have to come to God perfectly. We are supposed to bring him our broken parts so we can be renewed through the blood of Jesus.

72

There is literally no reason not to pray, and yet it took me years to understand the value of prayer. The value of bringing our burdens to God and trusting him. Surrendering our ways so we can receive peace in a time of brokenness is priceless. When we do not reach out to God in prayer, we find ourselves empty and void of God's direction.

If we are not seeking him while TTC, he cannot give us the answers we need until we trust him and add faith to the equation.

If we trust God, we will be in constant prayer, in constant search of his guidance, and constant in following his direction.

Rejoice in Hope

Usually when we think about rejoicing, it is because we have something to be joyful about. But in Romans 12:12, we are called to rejoice in the hope of something we have not yet received.

In Romans 8:24–25, hope is clearly defined: "...Now hope that is seen is not hope. For who hopes for what he sees? But if we hope for what we do not see, we wait for it with patience."

While TTCTF, we are hoping to get pregnant, and we are suppose to rejoice in that hope. If we are not rejoicing in the hope of conception we are failing to follow Romans 12:12.

In order to rejoice in hope, we have to make sure our hope is in God. We need our hope to be in the certainty of his abilities and his promises. Once our hope is properly aligned with God's will, we can rejoice in the hope of getting pregnant.

This joy will only come if we have complete faith and trust in God, his Word, and his promises.

When We Do Not Trust

God fulfills his promises based on faith and his Word. Not fear or deadlines, not anger or resentment, not false hope or what doctors say; he wants our faith and trust.

Do not let the pain and frustration of not having a child yet cloud your walk with God and further delay your blessings.

REFLECTION AND PRAYER TIME
· ·

1. Facing Tribulations

When we face tribulations, we can either grow bitter because of our circumstances or we can look to God, see his grace and mercy, and trust him to answer our prayers.

In Hebrews 12:15 (NIV) we see that our bitterness has roots and grows: "See to it that no one falls short of the grace of God and that no bitter root grows up to cause trouble and defile many."

Eliminate these bitter roots by seeking out the things that frustrate you; maybe it is waiting, marriage issues, or financial struggles. Anything that can cause bitterness needs to be cut off so our roots do not cause trouble.

The answer to all of our tribulations is to trust God because he is equipped to handle anything we are facing. He is a God worth trusting.

Psalm 86:15 says, "But you, O Lord, are a God merciful and gracious, slow to anger and abounding in steadfast love and faithfulness."

2. Praying No Matter What

No matter what your circumstances are, keep seeking God, drawing near to him, honoring him, and growing your faith in him. Do not make the mistake I did by forgetting this is a two-way relationship.

God wants all of you.

He does not want to be our genie who grants us wishes. He wants to bless us according to his Word. Let him do so by drawing near to him through prayer and obeying his Word.

3. Renewing Hope

Hope is about trust, and if you have been burnt out by hoping, I completely understand not wanting to let your guard down and be hopeful again.

Thankfully, hope in God will never let you down. Hoping in our Heavenly Father is unlike any other hope we have had before.

He is our God, and he does not break promises. We are the ones who stand in his way to bless us. When we get out of God's way by aligning our will with his will, there will be an abundance of blessings greater than we could have ever imagined.

That is worth hoping for.

PRAYER

· · · · · · ·

God, in my imperfection you wait. In my frustration, you wait. In my disobedience, you wait. As this life goes by, you continue to wait, Lord.

You are the God of love, who is patient and kind. In my waiting, I have been just the opposite. I have grown resentful, bitter, and my heart has hardened.

It hurts to keep feeling such a deep longing. It hurts to know that you are not answering this prayer even though I know you can. But, God, it hurts even more to realize that you want to bless me with a baby and I have held you back. Instead of digging deeper into you, I drifted further away. I have separated myself from you in my pain.

I have let my wants, desires, and dreams affect my relationship with you. I am sorry, God. Please restore this bitter, broken heart.

God, I know you are the same yesterday, today, and forever. I also know that my ways are not your ways, and my thoughts are not your thoughts. I know if you are waiting, you have a reason.

I will trust in your timing. I will trust in your purpose for this season. I will grow.

Please search my heart, God. Show me how to trust you. Show me how to dig deeper. Show me where I am outside of your will so I can get back on your path.

Thank you, God, for your patience in waiting on me. I love you, Lord.

In Jesus' name,
Amen

Chapter 11

IMPERFECT ACTION

The process of seeking God completely to get pregnant demands a lot of work, and I know it can be overwhelming.

We have addressed eliminating fear and walking in faith, finding peace in frustration, having patience in waiting, relying on God instead of ourselves, fighting our very thoughts that turn us from God, and so much more.

This process addresses our faults and our sins. We are searching ourselves to see where we need to be more in line with God and his Word.

God reveals our sins so we can correct them. Our sins will not go away overnight. The sinful world we live in constantly tries to pull us away from God's plan.

We have to fight this fight and know there will always be more work to be done because we will never be perfect. We will never clear all of the sin out of our lives. But when we try, when we give everything we can to God, he will bless our commitment.

I know other women do not have to surrender so much before they can receive this gift. I know the overwhelming frustration when other women seem to easily get pregnant while we have to beg, plead, and be diligent in giving it all to God. My answer to these frustrations is to focus on our own circumstances and work on our relationship with God.

I waited seven years to get pregnant. I even gave up on the hope of being a mom. I honestly thought God did not care about my hurt and pain. But those were lies, and those lies grew because I was not trusting and hoping in him.

I had to take responsibility for my sins and start taking action to eliminate them. James 1:23–25 shows us, "For if anyone is a hearer of the word and not a doer, he is like a man who looks intently at his natural face in a mirror. For he looks at himself and goes away and at once forgets what he was like. But the one who looks into the perfect law, the law of liberty, and perseveres, being no hearer who forgets but a doer who acts, he will be blessed in his doing."

We need to stop getting overwhelmed with the failures, the brokenness, and the mountain of problems we are facing and focus on what we can make right. We cannot make anything right if we are not putting the effort in. The Bible shows us over and over that we need to take action.

We may be victims of circumstance, doubt, or fear but I promise you, God is so much bigger than our biggest mountain.

With words, God formed us. He crafted the details of our bodies down to the tiniest specifications. He is bigger and greater than anything we will ever face. Trusting in him is what this journey is really about. We need to grow our faith in all circumstances and pursue a closer relationship with him.

God was giving me areas to work on while I was waiting, which gave me even greater hope. I felt God directing me back to his path, to be able to conceive.

I know God is perfect. By getting myself right with him, I knew there would be fruit from my efforts. I saw my sins as obstacles to receiving the gift of our child. With the hope of God blessing us with a baby, my drive to overcome these obstacles became stronger.

We all have different obstacles to overcome, there is not a one-size-fits-all solution to God answering our prayers. We are each gifted with a personal relationship with God. What comes easily to some is a challenge for others. I do know that God cares about you and wants this blessing for you. His design was specifically made for women to get pregnant and grow a healthy baby.

I know this season is for a purpose and that it will be used for his glory. If God wants you to walk through these steps to get pregnant, it is because he loves you and wants your relationship with him to grow deeper.

Even with all the promises of goodness to come from this season, I know it is still difficult. In Hebrews 12:7–11 (NIV), we receive very important insight about enduring hardship: "Endure hardship as discipline; God is treating you as his children. For what children are not disciplined by their father? If you are not disciplined—and everyone undergoes discipline—then you are not legitimate, not true sons and daughters at all. Moreover, we have all had human fathers who disciplined us and we respected them for it. How much more should we submit to the Father of spirits and live! They disciplined us for a little while as they thought best; but God disciplines us for our good, in order that we may share in his holiness. No discipline seems pleasant at the time, but painful. Later on, however, it produces a harvest of righteousness and peace for those who have been trained by it."

If we are willing to see God's discipline as a sign that something is not right with our walk, we can grow and learn from it.

This scripture shows us that the hardship and pain we face is for a reason. It is even beneficial for us. If we accept this training and endure it, we will be rewarded.

This is not pleasant, and God knows it, because it says so in Hebrews 12:11. However, we need to accept this discipline since we are not perfect so that we can learn and grow.

If we do not honor God through this season, we are rebelling and will miss out on the training God wants us to have. When I finally accepted God's discipline, the training I received prepared me in the most amazing ways to be a parent. Parenting takes patience, steadfastness, and reliance in God. All traits I did not have when we first were TTC.

Despite all of the work I put in, I am still not perfect but God continues to bless me. This difficult season showed me how to seek God for answers by modeling Jesus. Now I model this in my parenting, so our son can see we are not only hearers of the Word but also doers.

I am so grateful for these pre-parenting lessons of patience and reliance on God that this season produced in me. Many parents have to learn these lessons through sleepless nights. They have to work harder to find the balance they were not challenged with before they got their BFP (Big Fat Positive).

I can honestly tell you, after struggling for years, it has been a blessing—a blessing to my relationship with God, to my perspective as a mom, and to my marriage. This season ends with God honoring his Word because we honor him. The fruit of our obedience is always better than we can imagine.

Luke 16:15 shows us that "God knows your hearts." This can also be found in Psalm 44:21 and Romans 8:27. If the desire of our hearts is to honor God and we continue to align our will with his will, we will be blessed even through imperfect action.

Do not be overwhelmed by perfection. We all fall short, but we still need to take action. Seek the Lord, draw near to him, and follow his will. Failure is okay because it reveals where to grow in our relationship with God.

REFLECTION AND PRAYER TIME

· ·

1. Take Action

We are not perfect and God knows it, but we still have to take action. Do not worry about how difficult it is to overcome sin, just put the effort in, knowing God sees your heart and cares about your effort.

When you do the work, your actions will align you with James 1:23–25 so you have the proper training for the next season in your life.

2. Fruit From a Difficult Season

All seasons of life should produce fruit, including the most difficult seasons.

Galatians 6:9 shows us why we should not give up, "And let us not grow weary of doing good, for in due season we will reap, if we do not give up."

3. Remembering God Loves You

Please remember, God loves you. Through faith in him we can hope and rejoice. His Word shows us in Romans 5:5, "and hope does not put us to shame, because God's love has been poured into our hearts through the Holy Spirit who has been given to us."

Lean on God to get you through this season because he loves you.

PRAYER

· · · · · · ·

God, knowing that I am going to fail scares me. I do not want to fail. I do not want to be outside of your will.

I feel like I am already starting from behind. I desperately need you to fill the void of my shortcomings. My heart aches to serve you wholeheartedly, but my flesh fails constantly.

I reach for mountains and end up in a pit, but you, my God, are the God who moves mountains. Your clarity and your peace are worth searching for. Your love and your direction are the only guides I need in this life. I know you sent Jesus because you know of my faults and failures.

Through faith, not perfection, I see all things are possible.

My faith in you continues to grow, and I will keep taking action to align my will with your will.

I continue to hope in your plans and purpose in this imperfect life. I am completely trusting that in my weakness, you will shine the brightest.

Please use my weaknesses for your glory so that in my efforts to obey your Word, I can receive your blessings.

Thank you, Lord, for using this season to produce a closer relationship with you, for pregnancy, and for helping me to be a godly parent.

Your perfection makes all of this possible. Thank you, God.

In Jesus' name,
Amen

Chapter 12

BIBLICAL INFERTILITY

We cannot forget about the many times in the Bible when God opened the wombs of barren women.

Psalm 113:9 tells us, "He gives the barren woman a home, making her the joyous mother of children. Praise the LORD!"

This chapter is about biblical evidence. We are shown over and over again that God answers our prayers. To be able to look into the Word and see our specific prayers being answered so many times should give us the confidence, trust, and faith we need to believe God will answer our prayers of conception.

Here are seven women who have suffered like us. They were unable to get pregnant, and God answered their prayers with conception.

Sarah

Genesis 18:10–12: "The LORD said, 'I will surely return to you about this time next year, and Sarah your wife shall have a son.' And Sarah was listening at the tent door behind him. Now Abraham and Sarah were old, advanced in years. The way of women had ceased to be with Sarah. So Sarah laughed to herself, saying, 'After I am worn out, and my lord is old, shall I have pleasure?'"

Genesis 21:1–2: "The LORD visited Sarah as he had said, and the LORD did to Sarah as he had promised. And Sarah conceived and bore Abraham a son in his old age at the time of which God had spoken to him."

Rebekah

Genesis 25:21: "And Isaac prayed to the LORD for his wife, because she was barren. And the LORD granted his prayer, and Rebekah his wife conceived."

Rachel

Genesis 30:22–23: "Then God remembered Rachel, and God listened to her and opened her womb. She conceived and bore a son and said, 'God has taken away my reproach.'"

Manoah's Wife

Judges 13:2–3: "…And his wife was barren and had no children. And the angel of the LORD appeared to the woman and said to her, 'Behold, you are barren and have not borne children, but you shall conceive and bear a son.'"

Judges 13:24: "And the woman bore a son and called his name Samson. And the young man grew, and the LORD blessed him."

Hannah

1 Samuel 1:5: "But to Hannah he gave a double portion, because he loved her, though the LORD had closed her womb."

1 Samuel 1:20: "And in due time Hannah conceived and bore a son, and she called his name Samuel, for she said, 'I have asked for him from the LORD.'"

The Shunammite Woman

2 Kings 4:14: "…'Well, she has no son, and her husband is old.'"

2 Kings 4:16–17: "And he said, 'At this season, about this time next year, you shall embrace a son.' And she said, 'No, my lord, O man of God; do not lie to your servant.' But the woman conceived, and she bore a son about that time the following spring, as Elisha had said to her."

Elizabeth

Luke 1:6–7: " And they were both righteous before God, walking blamelessly in all the commandments and statutes of the Lord. But they had no child, because Elizabeth was barren, and both were advanced in years."

Luke 1:13–14: " But the angel said to him, 'Do not be afraid, Zechariah, for your prayer has been heard, and your wife Elizabeth will bear you a son, and you shall call his name John. And you will have joy and gladness, and many will rejoice at his birth…'"

Luke 1:24: "…Elizabeth conceived…"

REFLECTION AND PRAYER TIME

· ·

1. Read the context.

These scriptures get right to the point of the story, but please read the context of each story.

Second Timothy 3:16 says, "All Scripture is breathed out by God and profitable for teaching, for reproof, for correction, and for training in righteousness..."

God has been answering barren women's prayers since biblical times.

Find comfort and hope in these stories, and know that God is the answer to your prayers.

Let the Word guide you as you seek God to bless you.

2. Do not forget to hope.

Hoping in God and being certain of his abilities means no matter how long you have waited, no matter what your circumstances are, God can bless you to conceive a child.

If we do not have hope, we are doubting, and if we are doubting, we are not standing on faith.

PRAYER

· · · · · · ·

Thank you, God, for your Word and for reminding me that you are the God who answers prayers. You are the God who has no limitations.

Thank you for caring about my broken heart, and thank you for being able and willing to answer this prayer. I want to honor and obey you with my life.

Please show me your will.

Please reveal what I can do to get pregnant. Reveal when I am listening to lies so I can find your truth in all of my thoughts and actions. Show me how infertility is not an obstacle for you.

I commit to obeying your direction and honoring you completely.

I trust you, I hope in you, and I am committed to serving you.

Please restore the joy and hope in my heart.

Please open my womb and allow me to conceive a baby as you have done for Sarah, Rebekah, Rachel, Manoah's wife, Hannah, the Shunammite woman, and Elizabeth. I believe you have shown me over and over again that you have authority over the womb to restore my hope in answering this prayer.

Thank you, Lord, for hearing my prayers and loving me even through my struggles.

I love you, God!

In Jesus' name,
Amen

Chapter 13

HE IS FAITHFUL

Any emotional journey has its ups and downs. For some, it can be a strengthening experience, and for others, it can be a breaking experience. In my journey to become pregnant, I have experienced both. The broken, empty, settling place of what I believed to be true was where I stayed for years. I now know that was not God's plan. His Word is clear. His love is clear, and the fact that our life has purpose is clear.

When we accept the Lord into our hearts and give him authority over our lives, it is a wonderful dedication, but it is challenging. God's desire for us to grow is evident in our daily lives. If everything were easy, we would have no reason to dig deeper, pray harder, or fast longer. Thankfully, we serve a good God. A God of love, patience, and kindness. A God who answers our prayers.

After several years of trying to get pregnant, our third month of TTCTF, I only ovulated for one day. The day before was negative and the day after was negative on my ovulation tests. This meant we had one opportunity to conceive. We took advantage of that positive ovulation test and prayed for God's blessing. We talked very little about it for the next two weeks.

I had faith and my husband had faith. We felt if we dwelled on whether or not we were pregnant, we would go out of our minds. We knew what God was capable of. We knew he heard our prayers. We knew our faith continued to grow, and our hope was in him.

I personally put very little thought into the possibility of being pregnant those two weeks. I just felt like I did not need to keep asking. I knew God would either allow it to happen this month or he wouldn't. Time would let us know. The decision was already made, and I could not change it by wondering or worrying.

We prayed, we believed, we stood in faith, and we waited.

So cramps started about five days before my period was due. This is a regular sign for me that my period is coming. When the cramps continued the next two days, I decided to tell my husband to be prepared. I felt like my period was coming.

I really felt like the previous month, we were blindsided by a "no," and I did not want that to happen again. My husband and I were bummed but believed God had a reason for his timing. We knew there was more we could do in the meantime to prepare for pregnancy. We were not stuck waiting with nothing to do. We knew we could still be proactive in our walk of faith.

We were certain this was not a door shutting.

On Saturday, November 8, 2014, I woke up, opened my Bible, and read James 1. There is a lot of great scripture in this chapter. The beginning talks about enduring trials through faith, which I felt was very relevant to our current situation.

I had been battling to try to get pregnant, feeling like this whole season was a trial. I had hated the trial in the past, and now I was grateful. It had put me in this exact moment. I knew I could lean on the Lord, not just with words but with my actions. I was renewed in knowing that I did not have to have fear but could stand on faith, knowing the months and years of no's were because we were TTC without faith.

James 1:2–5 (NIV) says to "Consider it pure joy, my brothers and sisters, whenever you face trials of many kinds, because you know that the testing of your faith produces perseverance.

Let perseverance finish its work so that you may be mature and complete, not lacking anything. If any of you lacks wisdom, you should ask God, who gives generously to all without finding fault, and it will be given to you."

I easily related to enduring trials, which this scripture had talked about, but what now rang true in this scripture was about feeling complete. Complete is a word most women do not feel when they are TTC. However, when we endure through faith, it is possible to feel complete, even with an empty womb. When we believe, standing on his Word, continuing to grow and hope, then we can be complete, lacking nothing.

After my daily Bible reading, I decided I wanted to try a pregnancy test. My period was due in two days, but I just felt like it was time to try. As I got out that pregnancy test, I stopped myself. The past two months I had planned to wait until after my period was due. I could not figure out why I was getting ahead of myself. But I felt peace about it; I did not feel frantic.

I didn't have anything to drink yet and had already peed in the morning. I thought I might not even have enough to test. I decided to pee in a plastic cup, and it was just enough to test. I set my timer to five minutes. I dipped the stick in the little cup, waited the five seconds for it to absorb, laid the stick flat, and started my timer.

As the timer counted, I thought about what I would do if we were pregnant. I would wait to tell my husband in a special way somehow, later that night. I was planning all of this in my head, and one minute went by.

I glanced down at the test without expectation, knowing that five minutes were not up. As I viewed this test, the control line was thick and dark like I have seen before. But next to it was a faint line. My eyes widened and my heart jumped. What did this mean? I had never seen this before!

I remembered reading that it does not matter if the control is darker in a pregnancy test; the fact that you see another line makes it a BFP (Big Fat Positive). WHAT?! I did not have one of those fancy tests with words, so I thought I might be wrong. I thought my mind was playing tricks on me. I immediately got on my phone and searched my question.

Sure enough, it was true!

That faint line, which was growing darker by the second, meant we were pregnant. It was our BIG FAT POSITIVE! The five-minute timer was not even finished, and I knew. God answered our prayers! He blessed us through our faith, and the years of big fat no's did not matter anymore. We got our positive!

So how was I going to surprise my husband? The plan went out the window. I walked out of the bathroom holding the test and told him we were pregnant. I did not even wait for him to finish brushing his teeth. He was just as happy and joyful as I was.

We were finally able to celebrate.

Then we calculated a real due date, solidifying this reality into our lives. We were so grateful to the Lord. I spent years without faith in this area of my life, and now it was clear. Having faith in God was all we needed for our BFP.

It had been years of darkness, but we finally got to see the light, light which revealed what I needed to work on to receive this gift. God is our support in this life. We can choose to trust his Word and his truth or we can trust ourselves in our circumstances. I know for sure that without faith, we would have never received our BFP.

It is my hope and prayer you will be blessed with one too!

REFLECTION AND PRAYER TIME
• •

1. There is a way.

Know that with God, there is a way. While he is our Judge, he is also our Father who cares deeply for us and wants our trust and faith. He has given us free will to choose in this world.

If we choose to stand on his Word and be faithful, he will shine the light at our feet. He will guide us so we do not miss out on the blessings and promises his Word gives us.

2. Remember, this is a process.

The timeline is different for everyone, so keep at it. If you get discouraged, it is okay. Be honest with God. Use this book as a guide to remind you of areas to focus on so you can continue to grow closer to God.

Remember, when you draw near to him, he draws near to you. When you stop seeking, God starts waiting.

God can bless you while you are TTCTF. Just be certain you keep pursuing him.

PRAYER

• • • • • • •

God, throughout my doubt, my brokenness, my hurt, my pain, and my anger, you have been faithful. You have been faithful to me, to your Word, and to the promises you have given. You have never wavered. Even though I questioned and lost faith, you remained the same.

Now, God, my faith is growing, and my hope is solidifying in you, your plans, and your ways. Throughout this growth, you have continued to be patient, waiting for me to reach out and trust you.

I trust you, God.

I trust you hear this prayer and you are continuing to work in me.

I trust you will continue to guide me and show me where I need to grow and what I need to do to obey your Word. I trust you will answer this prayer according to your Word to get pregnant.

Please, God, open this womb; let me conceive a child. Let this child be completely healthy, grow to full term, and come out at your timing, ready to face this world with parents who are renewed in their faith and love for you.

Let all of the brokenness I have endured be replaced with the everlasting joy of motherhood. You have remained faithful in my unfaithfulness. I am so excited to see what you are able to do in my faith.

Thank you, God, for hearing and answering my prayers.

Thank you for being the God of miracles.

Thank you for your great love for me.

Thank you for renewing my hope and faith.

Thank you, God, for showing me where I was holding your hands back from blessing me. Thank you, God, for forgiving me.

I truly love you, Lord. You are the King on the throne, and your greatness is beyond anything I could imagine. I am in awe that something so big to me is something so easy for you. I love you and I will continue to walk in faith, trusting your timing.

To you, God, be the glory, forever and ever,
Amen

THANK YOU

Thank you so much for taking the time to read this book. I pray to our God in Heaven, who created us, that this book will be a tool to help you ultimately reach your goal of becoming pregnant and to have a deeper walk with the Lord.

God is our answer, and his Word is the greatest gift for instruction and direction.

Do not accept no unless God says no!

PRAYERS
. . . .

This book is full of prayers designed to help guide you as you are TTCTF. I have recorded all of the prayers so you can listen to them daily to help you grow and encourage your walk with God.

Download them for **free** at ttctf.com/resources.

CONNECT WITH ME
. . . .

I would love to hear from you!

Visit my website below to connect with me through the TTCTF Support Group. Here you can also send an email and join my newsletter to stay connected with me.

ttctf.com/resources.

I look forward to seeing God work in you during this season and hearing your testimony of a successful pregnancy!

EXTRAS

COMPASSION INTERNATIONAL

Did you know by purchasing this book you have helped save the lives of children around the world? My husband and I decided early on when writing this book that 50% of the proceeds would go back to the kingdom of the Lord.

The Bible talks clearly about honoring God with our blessings, including financial blessings, in Proverbs 3:9: "Honor the LORD with your wealth and with the firstfruits of all your produce."

Below is a short story of how we chose Compassion International to help be a part of growing God's kingdom and honoring him with our financial blessings.

In our walk, we all have our strengths and weaknesses. When my husband and I learned about tithing, it was a simple act of obedience that we never questioned. We knew God had blessed us, and we wanted to honor his blessing by giving back what is his. It had always been black and white to us until we were challenged by what our tithe was actually going toward.

We always tithed to the church we attended, so we felt we had fulfilled our responsibility to the Lord. The problem was, the churches we attended were not being responsible with our tithe. They were in debt, and most of that money went toward trying to get out of debt rather than reaching out to those in need.

This is not true of all churches. I know there are many churches that focus on giving back to the community, serving and shining God's light in their local areas. We were not fortunate to be a part of a church like that, which is why we became conscious tithers. After a lot of research, we believe our tithing dollars do so much more through Compassion than they ever have before.

Compassion has several areas of ministry that do tremendous good around the world. Together, with your order of this book, we are supporting the Child Survival Program by donating 50% of the proceeds from this book.

The Child Survival Program is a wonderful program designed to support pregnant mothers by giving them one-on-one pregnancy coaching and parenting support.

They provide pre- and post-natal visits, birth assistance, basic needs for the baby that include diapers, blankets, clothing, and hygiene. They even provide nutritional support and clean water.

Most importantly, these centers provide spiritual guidance through gospel-focused relationships with local church staff, who emphasize how Jesus is the way, the truth, and the light.

While we struggled through waiting in hopes of getting pregnant, many of these women will suffer horrible circumstances if we do not step in and help—not just so they survive but so they and their children thrive.

We are incredibly grateful for your support in this critical mission and know the Lord will bless your efforts.

Find out more information on this wonderful program at the link below.

www.ttctf.com/resources

There are always more children and mothers in need. If you would like to give more, they have a suggestion of supporting one of their centers for only $20 USD a month, which is approximately $0.67 a day.

Thank you so much!

WHY JESUS

I did not always believe there was one way, one truth, and one light. In fact, I believed it was impossible for there to be one God, the creator of everything, who also cares about me. In an ocean of people more meaningful and important than I felt, I could not imagine the God who created the universe could possibly be able to make time for me.

I did not believe I was much of anything, just a kid struggling to find purpose in what seemed like a meaningless life. For a long time I believed I could never be valued by anyone, especially when I was so small in such a big world.

A friend started bringing me to church, and I met the youth pastor. He always had answers to my questions. What amazed me was how the answers were easily found in the Bible. I had previously attended a church where most of my questions were answered with "We will find that out when we die." But God actually provides us with so many answers in the Bible; we just have to read it to get the answers.

Those biblical answers continue to be relevant to our lives today because it is the living Word of God, as it says in Hebrews 4:12: "For the word of God is living and active, sharper than any two-edged sword, piercing to the division of soul and of spirit, of joints and of marrow, and discerning the thoughts and intentions of the heart."

I learned who God really was as my questions were answered in the Bible. I discovered God loves us like a perfect Father. He is always there for us, even in our disobedience.

Even before I knew him, he knew me.

He crafted us in the womb and has a plan for our lives. He is all-knowing and all-seeing. He cares about us and wants what is best for us. That is why he has given us rules about how to live that we find in the Bible. He has given us instruction and wisdom to get the most out of this life.

He is not trying to be a mean daddy by telling us what is good and bad for us. He has given this loving instruction to bring us peace in our spirit.

> **"...God our Savior, who desires all people to be saved and to come to the knowledge of the truth."**
>
> **1 Timothy 2:3–4**

I was not an easy convert. I questioned everything and that was okay. God does not want us to change our minds like the wind; He wants our committed hearts. So seek him, and he will reveal himself to you.

Now I see how impossible it would be to believe in anything other than our Heavenly Father as our Creator, Protector, Provider, and Comforter.

When I thought I did not matter, it was because I looked around and saw how big and important and complicated everything was. But when I started to look at God, he revealed he was bigger and more important than everything we could see or fathom. I saw that he gives us his time, listens to us, and directs us. When I look to him I can no longer think I am insignificant because he has shown me over and over that we matter to him.

God remains faithful in our unfaithfulness, broken hope, pain, hurt, and confusion because he knows we need to learn, grow, and accept that we need him in this life. He will never disappoint us.

When the brokenness and heartache of silence and emptiness keep tearing you down, God will be there waiting for you to trust in his greatness.

Titus 2:11–12 (NIV)

"For the grace of God has appeared that offers salvation to all people. It teaches us to say 'No' to ungodliness and worldly passions, and to live self-controlled, upright and godly lives in this present age..."

2 Peter 3:9

"The Lord is not slow to fulfill his promise as some count slowness, but is patient toward you, not wishing that any should perish, but that all should reach repentance."

Luke 18:27 (NIV)

"Jesus replied, 'What is impossible with man is possible with God.'"

Matthew 7:13–14

"Enter by the narrow gate. For the gate is wide and the way is easy that leads to destruction, and those who enter by it are many. For the gate is narrow and the way is hard that leads to life, and those who find it are few."

Romans 10:10 (NIV)

"For it is with your heart that you believe and are justified, and it is with your mouth that you profess your faith and are saved."

John 3:16-17 (NIV)

"For God so loved the world that he gave his one and only Son, that whoever believes in him shall not perish but have eternal life. For God did not send his Son into the world to condemn the world, but to save the world through him."

1 Peter 2:24

"He himself bore our sins in his body on the tree, that we might die to sin and live to righteousness. By his wounds you have been healed."

1 John 1:9

"If we confess our sins, he is faithful and just to forgive us our sins and to cleanse us from all unrighteousness."

RECEIVING FORGIVENESS

Because of Jesus, we can easily receive God's forgiveness for our sins and receive all of the blessings he promises in his Word.

If you agree with Romans 10:9, which says, "...if you confess with your mouth that Jesus is Lord and believe in your heart that God raised him from the dead, you will be saved," then that is all you have to do. Acknowledge and confess through faith to receive forgiveness.

If you have never accepted Jesus Christ as your Lord and Savior, you are one prayer away from receiving the gift of salvation.

Please take a moment to reflect on the scriptures in this chapter, and if you believe this all to be true, say the salvation prayer on the next page.

PRAYER FOR SALVATION

· · · · · · · · · · · · · · · · · · · ·

God, my Creator, who formed me in the womb, please forgive me for living outside of your will. I want to honor you and glorify you in this life and obey your Word.

Please, God, forgive me of my sins through the blood of Jesus.

Let your Spirit lead me to honor you, and help me to stay far from sin. Thank you for loving me, caring for me, and guiding me.

Thank you for protecting me even before I knew you. I know you have a plan and purpose for my life.

Thank you for making me complete.

You are my God and King. You are Holy and righteous and good. Even though I am unworthy, you have loved me unconditionally, and I am so grateful for your grace and mercy, God.

Thank you for restoring my relationship with you through my faith in Jesus.

I love you, God!

In Jesus' name,
Amen

WHAT IS NEXT?

• • • • • • • • • • • •

Your life will never be the same now that you have God's forgiveness. I am so excited to see what God has in store for you!

2 Corinthians 5:17 says, "Therefore, if anyone is in Christ, he is a new creation. The old has passed away; behold, the new has come."

It may seem surreal to say a prayer and be forgiven for everything we have ever done wrong, but that is what the blood of Jesus has done for us. His sacrifice sets us free from sin.

Unfortunately, we are in a sinful world and we will never be perfect, but we can learn from Jesus's example and continue to receive forgiveness when we do sin.

From here, it is important to read the Bible, pray, and grow in your walk with God.

The Bible is the living Word of God. Hebrews 4:12 says, "For the word of God is living and active, sharper than any two-edged sword, piercing to the division of soul and of spirit, of joints and of marrow, and discerning the thoughts and intentions of the heart."

Finding a Bible-believing church or small group can help fellowship with other believers who believe what you do and who can help guide and support your walk.

God is so good, and we are blessed beyond measure to see the truth and to know our Creator loves us more than we could ever imagine.

If you have wandered away from God's plan and believe it is time for recommitting to God, please pray the prayer below. Praise God for his forgiveness!

PRAYER FOR RE-COMMITMENT

• •

God, I humbly come before you today full of regret. I have known you, but I have not made our relationship a priority. I have been getting by in this life, but I have missed so much from you.

Please forgive me, God.

The fire you ignited in me when I first accepted you into my life has been reignited, and I do not want it to go out. I want it to burn for eternity. I want to continue to draw near to you, to know your voice, and to know your ways. I do not want to conform to this world. I want to be transformed through the blood of Jesus. Please, God, draw near to me. Show me your ways, and make my thoughts your thoughts. Make my will match your will.

I am hungry for more of you, God. I want to hold on tight and never let go. No matter what I face, God, you have never left my side. You have made me whole in my brokenness. You are the answer to all of my pain. You are the light when I am surrounded by darkness. You are my provider, my comforter, and even my friend.

I recommit my life to you, Lord. I commit to changing my ways to honor you. You have replaced my hurt and pain with love and joy. You have given me abundance when I deserved nothing. You are all that I need.

Thank you, God, for your unending love for me. I love you, Lord.

In Jesus' name,
Amen

I would love to hear from you!

Please reach out to me at ttctf.com/resources. I am here if you have any questions or would like to tell me your story.

BRICK BY BRICK

Almost two years after our son was born, my husband and I were struggling to make some important decisions. Knowing life is complicated, we were concerned about continually falling into the same trap of unsuccessful efforts.

We were challenged one night when it all came crashing around us. After praying and asking for revelation, I opened the Bible and read Psalm 127:1: "Unless the LORD builds the house, those who build it labor in vein. Unless the LORD watches over the city, the watchman stays awake in vain."

This is a very powerful scripture, and it weighed heavily on me. I had this visual of the amount of intimacy it would take to build a house with the Lord brick by brick, laying each one down by being God's hands, serving him.

Honestly, I was overwhelmed because without having this kind of intimacy, everything I do is in vain.

How can I apply this partnership with God to our circumstances?

I felt I would fall short, no matter what. How could I be that committed, making every step about serving God?

The next day, this was still heavy on my heart, and as we read and prayed, God started to reveal to me that I already have laid a house with him, brick by brick, before. I have walked hand in hand with the Lord by TTCTF. This led me to a list of actions I took which allowed God to be our focus to get pregnant.

I hope this list helps you as it did me. These ten steps illustrate how dedicated we need to be when looking to God for his blessings and answers to our prayers.

BUILDING WITH GOD
. . . .

1. Recognize we cannot do this without God.

2. Read the Bible and memorize relevant scriptures.

3. Seek God constantly for answers; do not be complacent.

4. Do not accept "no" from anyone other than God.

5. Be confident in God's promises.

6. Have faith in God even if things don't happen in your timing.

7. Dig deeper, do not doubt when obstacles arise.

8. Deal with "unrelated" sin because sin is all related to God.

9. Consistently grow closer to God.

10. Do not let your circumstances minimize God's power.

This list can be applied to any situation in our lives. But it is not easy to follow. This requires a major commitment to God.

We need to be consistent and relentless in our desire to honor God with our actions, thoughts, and circumstances.

With this list in mind, ask God, "How can today be different? What can I do better?"

If we grow each day, it is amazing how much can change in our thoughts and actions. Our consistency is key to building dependency in the Lord in all areas of our lives, including when we are TTCTF.
James 1:2–3 says, "Count it all joy, my brothers, when you meet trials of various kinds, for you know that the testing of your faith produces steadfastness."

In life, we will face trials. This is not the first and it will not be the last trial, but this scripture in James is more evidence of working through the trials to get to God's blessings. This scripture shows us that there is joy in the growth. There isn't joy in the trial itself, but it is in the purpose for the trial where we can find joy.

This growth, which produces steadfastness, will follow you into the next stage of your life. It will prepare you for what is to come, and that is certainly a helpful trait as a parent.

Use this list as a summary while you are TTCTF. Work on each step and grow. God will guide you, and I am so hopeful you will receive that Big Fat Positive!

I hope this list becomes your go-to list when searching for God's promises, especially when TTCTF.

FREE FOR YOU

Get These Free Resources:

- The TTCTF Facebook Support Group
- The "He Is Faithful" Mini Video Series
- Recorded Scriptures and Prayers From This Book
- Additional Resources to Help While You are TTCTF

www.ttctf.com/resources

*If this book has helped you in any way, please consider sharing your experience on Amazon through a review. It means a lot to me and will help encourage other women in the same situation to start TTCTF!

Be a part of the
Through Faith community

The TTCTF Community is growing every day and we want you to be apart of it!

We go through the entire book together as well as the TTCTF Journal.

What happens in the TTCTF Community?

- √ Stop being alone during infertility
- √ Find a renewed relationship with God
- √ Eliminate the lies and manipulation of the enemy
- √ Find complete Truth in this season
- √ Attain genuine hope and expectation
- √ Be supported on the hard days
- √ Be encouraged through revelations
- √ Celebrate your victories with us... and there are

MANY VICTORIES!

Learn more at **www.TTCTF.com**

Be sure to check out the TTCTF Journal as a companion book while you are TTCTF.

Download the first week for free here:
ttctf.com/resources

I want to hear from you! Please connect with me at:

ttctf.com/resources

Made in the
USA
Monee, IL